The Samurai

The Samurai

Swords, Shōguns and Seppuku

Ben Hubbard

For Mum

Cover illustrations
Front: A nineteenth-century woodblock print shows a *rōnin* deflecting arrows with his *naginata*. (Library of Congress); back: Samurai armour (Shutterstock © psamtik)

First published 2014

The History Press
The Mill, Brimscombe Port
Stroud, Gloucestershire, GL5 2QG
www.thehistorypress.co.uk

British Library Cataloguing in Publication Data.
A catalogue record for this book is available from the British Library.

ISBN 978 0 7509 5589 8

Typesetting and origination by The History Press
Printed in Great Britain

Contents

Introduction

Samurai were the ancient fighting class of Japan; a martial elite which ruled the country for over 700 years. From their early beginnings as barbarian-subduing soldiers, the samurai would rise to prominence as large warrior clans, powerful enough to wrest control from the very emperor they were charged with protecting. The samurai would go on to become an aristocratic caste and lived according to a strict code of honour called *bushidō*, or 'way of the warrior'. *Bushidō* advocated honour, loyalty, pride and fearlessness in combat, and those who broke the code were expected to kill themselves.

A samurai would showcase his *bushidō* virtues on the battlefield, seeking out a worthy enemy warrior to engage in one-to-one combat. To find a suitable opponent of equal rank and social standing, a samurai would call out his own name, position and accomplishments. When a response came, the warrior, adorned with flags and family crests, would once again yell out his name and charge into the fray.

The warriors would first engage each other in a mounted archery duel. This required a great amount of skill and training, as a rider had to release the reins to fire arrows while maintaining control of his horse. If neither party was victorious with the bow, they would dismount and continue fighting on the ground with swords, daggers and bare hands if necessary. This was a fight to the death, and contests between two famous samurai often created a pause in the fighting as soldiers from both sides watched. A samurai's achievements in war were of paramount importance: the victorious fighter would chop off his opponent's head and add it to his tally to be inspected later by his lord, *shōgun* or emperor.

Samurai would rather die than be defeated and those not killed on the battlefield would be expected to perform *seppuku*, more commonly known today as *hara-kiri* ('cutting the stomach'). The ritual still provides a grisly source of fascination for Westerners, even centuries after the tradition was outlawed in Japan. *Seppuku* was always committed as a display of honour: it prevented the dishonour of capture and decapitation by the enemy; it helped to restore honour to a disgraced samurai; and, when used as a form of capital punishment, it allowed a condemned warrior to die an honourable death. *Seppuku* is considered to be one of the most painful ways for a human to die, and the bravest samurai were considered to be those who created the largest gaping wound or, better still, left viscera hanging from it.

The bloodiest period of samurai history undoubtedly took place during Japan's medieval age (1185–*c*.1600), when bitter inter-clan conflicts and civil war wracked the country. It is ironic, then, that instances of *seppuku* actually increased in the seventeenth century, during an enforced period of peace. While the country prospered during this time, the ruling samurai class, which was paid a national dividend to stand battle-ready, became slowly defunct. Without wars to fight, warriors found themselves doing the unthinkable – taking employment as teachers, bureaucrats and umbrella makers. Other samurai became *rōnin* – masterless warriors destined to roam aimlessly around Japan, searching for work as hired hands and fighting with one another. *Seppuku* became a wholly common occurrence in the seventeenth century, used as both a form of capital punishment and a deterrent to keep bored samurai in check.

The bar for obligatory *seppuku* at this time was set painfully low – insulting a superior, harbouring Christians and brawling all received the same sentence of death by suicide. As a further hindrance to bad behaviour, a law was passed that made both parties in a violent argument equally responsible, regardless of what the dispute was about or who caused it. As the use of *seppuku* as capital punishment increased, so did the protocol for the elaborate ceremonies that surrounded it. For those about to die, white robes, final meals and paper for death poems were provided, as well as a nominated 'second' to perform decapitation before the pain became too great.

Instead of indulging in street scuffles and bar brawls, samurai were encouraged to turn their attention to more intellectual and spiritual pursuits – calligraphy, poetry, tea ceremonies and the teachings of Buddha. Numerous texts on *bushidō* were produced during this period, many of them reflective and highly philosophical. This literature mainly concentrated on what it meant to be a samurai warrior, rather than providing practical military applications of how to perform as one. The heroic exploits of great samurai were also recounted with wistful and romanticised flourishes; the most celebrated warriors were unshakably loyal, educated in the arts of war, indomitable on the battlefield and, oddly, often fated to lose. Fidelity until death was considered the most important *bushidō* virtue, and there was a particular appeal in the blindly obsequious samurai who had been betrayed and forced to become an outlaw.

Accounts of legendary samurai often crossed over into myth and fantasy, where warriors would battle supernatural creatures and even flee the shores of Japan for heroic exploits in foreign lands. Much of the information about the samurai stems from this peaceful period, where literature, woodblock prints and theatre provide tales often sentimentally told. In modern times, television, movies and video games have contributed to the view of the samurai as stoic and pure-hearted, able to cut down whole armies single-handedly. This anachronistic image is often perpetrated by Hollywood, whose portrayal of the pious, philosophical warrior in *The Last Samurai* was described by one Japanese reviewer as 'setting his teeth on edge'.

While movie-makers of the West grapple with complex alien cultures, it is the samurai's foreignness which gives their history such allure and exotic appeal. On the small islands of Japan, with little outside influence and centuries of isolation, one of the great martial orders of the world rose and fell. This is their history.

I

The Way of the Warrior

THE LEGENDARY SAMURAI

Perhaps the greatest samurai who ever lived was Miyamoto Musashi. He was something of an eccentric – he paid little attention to his appearance, was often described as 'unwashed' and was frequently late to his duelling bouts. Musashi was cultivated and accomplished in calligraphy, painting and sculpture, and had killed many men before he had left his teens. He was a swordfighting strategist and dispatched more warriors in duels than any other known samurai, often fighting with sticks, branches and even the oar from a boat. However, his skill with a samurai blade was such that he could split a grain of rice on a man's forehead without drawing blood.

Musashi recorded his accomplishments in *The Book of Five Rings*, a manual on swordfighting strategy:

I went from province to province duelling with strategists of various schools, and not once failed to win, even though I had as many as sixty encounters. This was between the ages of thirteen and twenty-eight or twenty-nine.[1]

Shinmen Musashi no Kami Fujiwara no Genshin was born in 1584, although he later took the name Miyamoto Musashi after his mother's clan. By the time he was 7 years old, both of his parents had died and Musashi went to be raised and educated by his uncle, Dorin. Musashi's first duel was against a travelling samurai called Arima Kihei, who had posted a public notice seeking opponents. Musashi wrote down his name and the challenge was accepted. Dorin was horrified by the news and tried to call off the duel by explaining to Kihei that his nephew was only 13 years old, but Kihei insisted that, for his honour to remain intact, the duel would have to proceed unless Musashi showed up at the scheduled time to prostrate himself. Instead, on the morning of the duel, Dorin arrived to apologise on Musashi's behalf. As this was happening, Musashi strode into the hall, grabbed a quarterstaff and charged at Kihei, killing him instantly.

Two years later, the 15-year-old Musashi embarked on a warrior pilgrimage of the country, and it did not take long for his reputation to reach mythological proportions – the young samurai had won more duels than anyone in the history of Japan. Musashi also seemed able to turn virtually any object into a lethal weapon, often favouring the wooden *bokken* over a steel sword.

At the age of 21 Musashi arrived in Kyoto, where he set about challenging the masters of the nearby Yoshioka school. He had soon killed every one of them, leaving only 12-year-old Matashichiro as head of the Yoshioka family. Despite the school's dwindling numbers, a challenge was issued to Musashi for a final duel at the Ichijoji Temple on Kyoto's outskirts, but instead of meeting another samurai warrior, Musashi was to be ambushed by the remaining Yoshioka clan, armed with bows and arrows, swords and arquebuses.

Up until that point, Musashi had been late for every one of the Yoshioka duels, much to the disgust of his opponents. On the day of the final duel, however, he arrived some hours early, suspecting he had pushed the Yoshioka family into a surprise act of retribution. Musashi hid himself and lay in wait. Soon afterwards, a number of armed warriors arrived to make preparations for their ambush. Musashi then leapt from his hiding place and slaughtered a path through the Yoshioka samurai to Matashichiro himself, whom he killed before escaping unharmed. The battle left the Yoshioka school without a leader, students or family – and certainly without a reputation.

At the age of 28, Musashi fought his most legendary duel against his deadliest opponent yet – samurai master Sasaki Kojirō, who was known for his skill with a long straight sword, or *nodachi*, which he called 'the laundry drying pole'. Kojirō taught swordplay at his school, where students would learn his signature stroke – the 'swallow cut'. This consisted of a horizontal slashing movement that was so fast and precise that it looked like a swallow's tail in flight. Kojirō was known to have killed many foes with this stroke.

The duel had been scheduled for the morning of 3 April 1612 on Funajima Island. Musashi was running late as usual, and there was no sign of him or his boat as Kojirō paced the island's shore. Musashi had overslept and, when finally roused, he only had time to run to the boat which was waiting to row him to the island. However, as soon as the boat set off, Musashi realised that he was only carrying his short *wakizashi* sword and had left his main *katana* sword behind. Instead of turning back, the samurai set about carving himself a *bokken* from a spare oar as the boat continued across the water.

Kojirō's fury at his opponent's late arrival quickly turned to mirth when he saw Musashi's crudely fashioned weapon, but Musashi did not appear ruffled by Kojirō's taunts and simply held his weapon forward as a sign to let battle commence. The bout was as short as it was decisive. Kojirō made the first move, charging at Musashi and unleashing his swallow cut, which came so close to Musashi's head that it sliced off his topknot. At the same moment, Musashi delivered a fatal blow with his oar. Kojirō fell forward onto his knees and then slumped backwards, his skull cracked open.

The episode represented the zenith of Musashi's duelling career, which he gave up, aged 30, for a quieter life of reflection:

> When I reached thirty I looked back on my past. The previous victories were not due to my having mastered strategy. Perhaps it was natural ability, or the order of heaven, or that other schools' strategy was inferior. After that I studied morning and evening searching for the principle, and came to realise the 'Way of Strategy' when I was fifty.[2]

Musashi retired to live in a cave at the age of 60, and it is here that he wrote *The Book of Five Rings*. He died in 1645 – his body found sitting bolt upright with his *wakizashi* at the ready in his belt.

Musashi has been the subject of countless plays, poems, movies and books, not just because of his duelling prowess, but because he was the paragon of the samurai ethos. His books on strategy swordplay and the philosophy of the 'way of the warrior' are still studied today.

BUSHIDŌ

Bushidō or the 'way of the warrior' was the code of ethics that every samurai was encouraged to live and die by. It advocated a martial spirit of courage and fearlessness, alongside the virtues of loyalty, honour, rectitude, respect, benevolence, obedience, honesty, duty, filial piety (duty to one's family and ancestors) and self-sacrifice. These ideals were heavily influenced by the belief systems of Buddhism, Zen, Confucianism and Shintō. Buddhism taught a warrior not to be scared of death, as he would be reincarnated in the next life. Zen helped a warrior 'empty his mind' and maintain clarity in battle. Confucianism encouraged morality and self-sacrifice. Finally, Shintō advocated loyalty, patriotism and ancestor-worship.

The ideology behind *bushidō* began its development from the ninth century onwards, when a warrior's most valued attributes were his military skills and fortitude in war. Nevertheless, it was not long before the samurai were expected to be more than just good fighters. The best warriors were eulogised in a twelfth-century war chronicle, the *Heike Monogatari* (*Tale of the Heike*), as self-sacrificing, dutiful, respectful and utterly devoted to their clan. By the fourteenth century, chivalric virtues began to make an appearance in Japanese texts and, from then on, samurai were encouraged to couple their courage and military prowess with kindness, frugality, honesty and rectitude. These principles became an integral part of the samurai code, which from the fifteenth century was known as *bushidō*.

This 'way' was often laid out for samurai in a simple set of rules and regulations, such as the following sixteenth-century *Precepts of Katō Kiyomasa*:

Codes which all samurai should follow, regardless of rank:

❖ One should not be negligent in the way of the retainer. One should rise at four in the morning, practise sword technique, eat one's meal, and train with the bow, the gun, and the horse. A well-developed retainer should become even more so.

❖ If one should want diversions, he should make them outdoor pastimes such as falconry, deer-hunting and wrestling.

❖ For clothing, anything between cotton and natural silk will do. A man who squanders money for clothing and brings his household finances into disorder is fit for punishment. Generally one should concern oneself with armour appropriate for his social position and use his money for martial affairs.

❖ When associating with one's ordinary companions, one should limit the meeting to one guest and one host, and the meal should consist of plain brown rice. When practising the martial arts, however, one may meet with many people.

✧ As for decorum at the time of a campaign, one must be mindful that he is a samurai. A person who loves beautification where it is unnecessary is fit for punishment.

✧ The practice of Noh Drama is absolutely forbidden. When one unsheathes his sword, he has cutting a person down on his mind. Thus, as all things are born from being placed in one's heart, a samurai who practises dancing, which is outside of the martial arts, should be ordered to commit *seppuku*.

✧ One should put forth great effort in matters of learning. One should read books concerning military matters, and direct his attention exclusively to the virtues of loyalty and filial piety. Reading Chinese poetry, linked verse, and *waka* [Japanese poetry] is forbidden. One will surely become womanised if he gives his heart knowledge of such elegant and delicate refinements. Having been born into the house of a warrior, one's intentions should be to grasp the long and the short swords and to die.

✧ If a man does not investigate the matter of *bushidō* daily, it will be difficult for him to die a brave and manly death. Thus it is essential to engrave this business of the warrior into one's mind well.

✧ The above conditions should be adhered to night and day. If there is anyone who finds these conditions difficult to fulfil, he should be dismissed, an investigation should be quickly carried out, it should be signed and sealed that he was unable to mature in the Way of Manhood, and he should be driven out. On this, there can be no doubt.[3]

In the seventeenth century, notions about what it meant to be a samurai would once again change. During this time, known as the Edo Period, *Shōgun* Tokugawa Ieyasu declared there would be 'no more wars' and hundreds of thousands of samurai became unemployed as a result. For centuries the samurai had been either fighting battles or on standby waiting for another to start. Many of these warriors now became *rōnin* – masterless samurai who wandered aimlessly around the Japanese provinces looking for work and getting into trouble. Samurai brawls and street fighting became a common occurrence and laws were passed to make such offences punishable by death. *Seppuku* was the standard form of capital punishment in such cases, which at least allowed a disgraced samurai the chance to die an honourable death.

Instead of causing a public nuisance, samurai were encouraged to fill their time with artistic and intellectual interests – calligraphy, poetry, tea ceremonies and the teachings of Buddha among them. The texts published on *bushidō* during this period included special emphasis on samurai conducting themselves as refined and cultivated warriors, with long sections on the new application of their martial principles in peacetime. These texts considered the samurai heroes of the past, and gave romanticised accounts of their 'great deeds' in an attempt to make warriors of the day behave more like their predecessors.

While many of the seventeenth-century *bushidō* texts were philosophical and theoretical, the most popular book of the period, *Hagakure*, proclaimed the 'way of the warrior' could only be found in death.

HAGAKURE

Hagakure (Fallen Leaves) was samurai Yamamoto Tsunetomo's version of *bushidō*, published some years after his death. *Hagakure* was a favourite among Edo Period warriors, as it was at odds with contemporary *bushidō* texts that focused on chivalry and gentlemanly values. Instead, *Hagakure* argued that a warrior's life should be devoted to one's master and the preparation for death:

> Although it stands to reason that a samurai should be mindful of the Way of the Samurai, it would seem we are all negligent. Consequently, if someone were to ask, 'What is the true meaning of the Way of the Samurai?' the person who would be able to answer promptly is rare. This is because it has not been established in one's mind beforehand. From this, unmindfulness of the Way can be known … The Way of the Samurai is found in death. When it comes to either/or, there is only the choice of death. It is not

particularly difficult. Be determined and advance. To say that dying without reaching one's aim is to die a dog's death is the frivolous way of sophisticates. When pressed with the choice of life or death, it is not necessary to gain one's aim.[4]

KENDO

Another consequence of the Edo Period of peace was the formation of hundreds of fencing schools around Japan. These were intended to further enhance the Edo message of education and discipline, while offering a practical outlet for their theory. Ironically, the schools would also serve as a beacon for wandering swordsmen who wished to challenge the head to a duel. Being the head of a fencing school was a good source of income for an unemployed samurai, but it had every chance of ending in disgrace if he was challenged and defeated by a *rōnin*. Inside the schools, students fought with wooden *bokken* swords and learned *kendo*, the 'way of the sword'. Like *bushidō*, *kendo* was a belief system that encouraged self-sacrifice and discipline, and it is still taught in many fencing schools around the world today.

A young samurai warrior would be brought up according to the 'way of the sword' and the 'way of the warrior', and from the age of 3 was given a wooden *bokken* to fight with. Training would begin at 5 years old, when the child warrior was presented with his first real blade. Then he would be instructed in basic combat by his father and brothers, before being sent away to the home of a fencing instructor. Trainee warriors would learn the military arts, including archery, horsemanship, swordfighting, unarmed combat and, from the sixteenth century onwards, how to handle firearms. In addition, the samurai would be versed in the theory of warfare and *bushidō*.

When a warrior turned 15 he was initiated into the samurai fold in the *genpuku* ceremony, where he was given an adult name, a sword and samurai armour. Every young warrior was expected to live a spartan existence to successfully become a samurai. As *Hagakure* states: 'It is said that one should rise at four in the morning, bathe and arrange his hair daily, eat when the sun comes up and retire when it becomes dark.' In addition to this mental preparation was the essential weapons training that would turn the samurai into a deadly fighting machine on the battlefield. To become truly accomplished, a samurai would need to be equally versed with the *naginata*, a polearm weapon, as with the bow, sword and arquebus. In *The Book of Five Rings*, Miyamoto Musashi summarises the virtues of each weapon:

> The bow is tactically strong at the commencement of battle, especially on a moor, as it is possible to shoot quickly from among the spearmen. However, it is unsatisfactory in sieges, or when the enemy is more than forty yards away ... From inside fortifications, the gun has no equal among weapons. It is the supreme weapon on the field before the ranks clash, but once swords are crossed the gun becomes useless ... The halberd [naginata] is inferior to the spear on the battlefield. With the spear you can take the initiative; the halberd is defensive ... Because bows, guns, spears and halberds are all warriors' equipment they are certainly part of strategy. To master the virtue of the long sword is to govern the world and oneself, thus the long sword is the basis of strategy. The principle is 'strategy by means of the long sword'. If he attains the virtue of the long sword, one man can beat ten men. Just as one man can beat ten, so a hundred men can beat a thousand, and a thousand can beat ten thousand. In my strategy, one man is the same as ten thousand, so this strategy is the complete warrior's craft.[5]

WEAPONS OF WAR

THE SWORD

The samurai sword was a warrior's most prized possession and would only leave his sight in death. It was the badge and privilege of the samurai class to bear arms and each warrior carried two swords, one long (the *tachi* and, later, the *katana*) and one short (the *wakizashi*). The swords would be with the samurai at all times and never more than an arm's length away during sleep. The *wakizashi* was not normally used for fighting, but instead to chop the heads off defeated warriors and to commit *seppuku*. The *katana* was made with a gentle curve and was perfectly balanced to enable a precise cutting action.

The forging of a new sword was considered a sacred art, and one which would take expert swordsmiths months to complete. Just to create the steel for a samurai sword was an arduous process, taking ten men over three days to smelt the carbon-rich steel pieces that would go on to be forged into a blade. To make the steel, iron-sand was poured into a 1,000°c charcoal furnace called a *tatara*. Over seventy-two hours the sand would form into pieces of crude steel, known as *tamahagane*. Once cooled, the best *tamahagane* pieces were sent to a swordsmith to begin the forging process.

A master swordsmith would make a new samurai blade over several weeks; his team would include smiths to forge the blade's shape, assistant smiths to fold the metal with hammers, a polisher, a blade expert, and sheath and hilt artisans. Every man involved would dress in white ceremonial clothes and perform Shintō rituals throughout the highly ceremonial process. The samurai blade was created with two types of steel: a softer, lower carbon steel in its centre; and harder, high carbon steel on the outside. These different types of steel were forged in a furnace reaching 1,300°c and then folded up to sixteen times through hammering, which distributed the carbon content evenly throughout the blade. The inner steel was then wrapped in the outer steel and welded together to form a 60–80cm blade. This bi-metallic construction was the true genius of the samurai sword – a combination of soft, flexible steel running through its core, wrapped in a hard cutting shell. The result was a razor-sharp cutting blade that could also absorb shock. This reduced the chances of the sword bending or snapping in combat, and also enabled it to be used as a shield, which samurai warriors did not carry.

Swordfighting technique was called *kenjutsu*, or the 'art of the sword'. A samurai would grasp the handle of his sword with both hands and train in the sixteen varieties of cut, most of which used a downward stroke. Young samurai practised their cuts on the bodies of criminals, either dead or alive, so they could experience slicing human flesh. Hours could be devoted to learning one move, such as the *Iaido* – a single, smooth movement that pulled the *katana* from its scabbard, struck down the opponent, wiped the blade clean of blood, and returned the sword to its sheath.

CUTS AND STROKES

It was considered important for a warrior to study the various swordfighting styles of different samurai masters, as each one practised their own methods and techniques. Miyamoto Musashi favoured a type of *kenjutsu* called *nitōjutsu*, or the 'two sword' method. In *The Book of Five Rings*, Musashi suggests: 'It is not difficult to wield a sword in one hand; the way to learn this is to train with two long swords, one in each hand. It will seem difficult at first, but everything is difficult at first.' In his book, Musashi also gave instructions about specific cuts and moves to be used in combat:

To Hit the Enemy in One Timing

'In One Timing' means when you have closed with the enemy to hit him as quickly and directly as possible, without moving your body or settling your spirit, while you see that he is still undecided. The timing of hitting before the enemy decides to withdraw, break or hit, is this 'In One Timing'.

Continuous Cut

When you attack and the enemy also attacks, and your swords spring together, in one action cut his head, hands and legs. When you cut several places with one sweep of the long sword, it is the 'Continuous Cut'. You must practise this cut, it is often used. With detailed practice you should be able to understand it.

Cut and Slash

To cut and to slash are two different things. Cutting, whatever form of cutting it is, is decisive, with a resolute spirit. Slashing is nothing more than touching the enemy. Even if you slash strongly, and even if the enemy dies instantly, it is slashing. When you cut, your spirit is resolved. You must appreciate this. If you first slash the enemy's hands or legs, you must then cut strongly. Slashing is in spirit the same as touching. When you realise this, they become indistinguishable. Learn this well.

Glue and Lacquer Emulsion Body

The spirit of 'Glue and Lacquer Emulsion Body' is to stick to the enemy and not separate from him. When you approach the enemy, stick firmly with your head, body and legs. People tend to advance their head and legs quickly, but their body lags behind. You should stick firmly so that there is not the slightest gap between the enemy's body and your body. You must consider this carefully.

To Scold 'Tut-TUT!'

Scold means that, when the enemy tries to counter-cut as you attack, you counter-cut again from below as if thrusting at him, trying to hold him down. With very quick timing you cut, scolding the enemy. Thrust up, 'Tut!', and cut 'TUT!' This timing is encountered time and time again in exchange of blows. The way to scold 'Tut-TUT' is to time the cut simultaneously with raising your long sword as if to thrust the enemy. You must learn this through repetitive practice.

The Flowing Water Cut

'The Flowing Water Cut' is used when you are struggling blade to blade with the enemy. When he breaks and quickly withdraws trying to spring with his long sword, expand your body and spirit and cut him as slowly as possible with your long sword, following your body like stagnant water. You can cut with certainty if you learn this. You must discern the enemy's grade.

There Are Many Enemies

'There Are Many Enemies' applies when you are fighting one against many. Draw both sword and companion sword and assume a wide-stretched left and right attitude. The spirit is to chase the enemies around from side to side, even though they come from all four directions. Observe their attacking order, and go to meet first those who attack first. Sweep your eyes around broadly, carefully examining the attacking order, and cut left and right alternately with your swords. Waiting is bad. Always quickly reassume your attitudes to both sides, cut the enemies down as they advance, crushing them in the direction from which they attack. Whatever you do, you must drive the enemy together, as if tying a line of fishes, and when they are seen to be piled up, cut them down strongly without giving them room to move.[6]

SECONDARY WEAPONS AND ARMOUR

The main samurai weapons used in conjunction with the sword were the bow, *naginata* and, later, the arquebus. During the early Heian Period, the bow was considered to be a samurai's primary weapon, as duels between warriors would always begin, and often end, with a mounted archery contest. The bow was specially designed to shoot an arrow from one third of the way up its shaft, which made it easier to fire on horseback. Bows were made from bamboo strips, glued together and wrapped with rattan, making them, strong, rigid and tremendously hard to pull back. Arrows were also fashioned from bamboo, covered with lacquer and tipped with steel arrowheads. There were many different types of arrowheads, including the famous whistling arrows used to signal the start of samurai hostilities. Each of these arrows, also known as 'humming-bulb' arrows, was fixed with a wooden head that whistled as it sailed through the air. Another arrowhead constructed in a 'V' shape was designed to disrobe a warrior by cutting the cords that held his armour in place.

The *naginata* was a 30–60cm curved blade attached to a long pole. This weapon was favoured by *ashigaru* (foot soldiers), *sōhei* (warrior monks) and women. The *naginata* grew to prominence during the Genpei War, when cavalry charges by mounted samurai were at their most common. With its curved blade and long reach, the *naginata* was at its most effective when used against an opponent on horseback. As such, the weapon helped to level the odds on the battlefield, giving the common foot soldier a chance against the well-equipped, mounted samurai.

Traditional samurai armour was known as *yoroi* – lamellar armour consisting of leather plates laced together with leather or silk cords. These plates would be treated with lacquer and put together using an overlapping technique to create strong, waterproof and lightweight armour. The armour had a rectangular piece, called a *dou*, that covered the chest and back. Hanging from the *dou* was a skirt, or *kusazuri*, that covered the wearer's upper legs. The *haidate* was added over the thighs, *suneate* covered the shins and *kogake* protected the feet. *Sode* was square-shaped shoulder protection, and *kote* was armoured sleeves that extended from the shoulders to the forearms

To protect the head, a samurai wore a helmet, or *kabuto*, which was constructed from up to a hundred leather or metal plates tightly lashed or riveted together. Hanging from the bottom of the *kabuto* was a *shikoro*, which protected the neck. Facial armour was called *mempo* and was attached to the *kabuto* with metal rods, and sometimes included a covering for the front of the throat. Helmets and masks became increasingly elaborate during samurai history, with some featuring sinister grinning mouths to intimidate opponents, and often a fake moustache. Ornaments that sat atop a samurai's helmet also became more ostentatious and included peacock feathers, antler horns, 'sunburst' crests and stylised centipedes.

Early Heian Period samurai armour was designed to protect and be flexible enough for the samurai to fire a bow from horseback. However, from the mid-sixteenth century, the introduction of firearms was to change Japanese warfare, and plate armour, chain mail and cuirasses made from iron and steel strips were introduced. This 'bullet-tested' armour, or *tameshi*, was used until the Edo Period, when the era of peace made battlefield armour redundant.

Samurai firearms were heavy and clumsy Portuguese arquebuses, which reached Japanese shores by way of a shipwreck in 1543. The arquebus employed the matchlock system, which required the user to light a long fuse that ran into a touch hole to spark the charge. This gave the soldier time to take aim before the weapon fired, unlike earlier versions which required a live match to be dropped into the touch hole.

The arquebus received a mixed response from the samurai. Many older veterans considered it offensive and dishonourable that such a clumsy weapon could be fired by a common *ashigaru* foot soldier to anonymously kill a samurai warrior. A samurai, after all, devoted his life to the ritual of warfare and training in the weaponry of one-to-one combat. An arquebus, on the other hand, could be used effectively by an *ashigaru* after only a few days' training. While this was judged the weapon's greatest disgrace, it was also its best asset in terms of battlefield domination. Clan leader Oda Nobunaga was quick to realise the weapon's potential and monopolised its use to become the first great unifier of Japan in the sixteenth century (see page 96). Nobunaga used the weapon to deadly effect across three firing lines, so multiple volleys could be let off against ranks of charging cavalry.

The devastating effectiveness of firearms against mounted, sword-wielding samurai would be brutally demonstrated at the end of the samurai era in 1877. Here, the American Gatling gun would be fired by a new Japanese conscript army against the rebel samurai leader, Saigō Takamori. Takamori and his warriors were slaughtered, proving that the mighty samurai sword was of little use against modern firearms.

NOTES

1   Miyamoto Musashi, *The Book of Five Rings*
2   Ibid.
3   *Precepts of Katō Kiyomasa*
4   Yamamoto Tsunetomo, *Hagakure: The Way of the Samurai*
5   Musashi, *The Book of Five Rings*
6   Ibid.

2

Seppuku

Seppuku was the samurai's form of suicide, often known as *hara-kiri* or 'cutting the stomach'. This involved cutting across the lower abdomen to expose the innards, and, in the cases considered bravest, leaving the entrails hanging from the wound. *Seppuku* is one of the most excruciating ways a person can die and, as such, was designed to provide a samurai warrior with an honourable death. It was also often committed to reduce shame, restore honour and nullify accusations of cowardice.

The act was first committed by samurai trapped in battle. Using a sword, dagger or any implement to hand, these warriors would take their own lives rather than face capture and execution by the enemy. Disgraced samurai would also use *seppuku* to show their contrition, and at other times as a form of protest against extreme wrongdoing. Later, samurai would commit *seppuku* to honour a dead master, or be condemned to perform the act as a form of punishment. At these times, *seppuku* would be committed as part of a highly ritualised ceremony, performed with the help of assistants in front of spectators.

Such ceremonies would begin with the samurai bathing, dressing in a white kimono, eating a final meal and writing a death poem. The warrior would then take up his blade and plunge it around 1in into the left-hand side of his abdomen, directly below the navel. He would then drag the blade around 6in to his right side and make a final pull upwards. It would take an agonisingly long time for a samurai to die from *seppuku* alone, so a second, or *kaishaku*, would be on hand to cut off the samurai's head at the correct moment. This was a difficult and thankless task – the *kaishaku* would gain no acknowledgment or credit for helping the samurai, but instead face ignominy if the task was bungled. To avoid the head flying off and hitting officials or rolling away, the *kaishaku* was advised to leave a flap of skin on the neck so the severed head could remain attached to the body. Another form of *seppuku* called *jūmonji giri* was performed without a second and used a vertical instead of a horizontal cut. The samurai was then expected to hold his hands over his face while he bled to death.

The act of *seppuku* was performed in an extraordinary variety of ways during the samurai period. There are some striking examples recorded in the various annals: a samurai slashes his stomach and throws his intestines against a wall; a 15-year-old boy slits his grandfather's wrists before slicing open his belly and falling dead on top of him; and a mounted warrior cuts open his stomach, flings his intestines to the ground, and then inserts his sword into his mouth before jumping face-first onto it. While the rationale for *seppuku* can often broadly be explained as maintaining or restoring honour, there are as many variations on this theme as instances of the act itself. Among the notably extreme examples are this stairway altercation in the early nineteenth century:

Two officers belonging to the Emperor's staff met upon the imperial staircase; their swords happened to entangle, and words arose. Said one to the other, coolly, 'It is only an accident, and at best it is only a quarrel between the two swords'. 'We shall see about that,' cried the other, excitedly; and with these words he drew his weapon and plunged it into his breast. The other, impatient to obtain the same advantage, hurried away upon some errand of service which he was slowly performing, and instantly returned to his antagonist, who was already at the point of death. On inquiring if he was still alive, and being informed of the fact, he also plunged his sword into his own body, exclaiming, 'You should not have had the start of me if you had not found me engaged in the service of the Prince. I die contented, however, since I have had the glory of convincing you that my sword is as good as yours.'[1]

SEPPUKU HISTORY

The act of *seppuku* was intrinsically Japanese and was modified, refined and perfected over 1,000 years of samurai history. However, its beginnings are obscure. It is unlikely *seppuku* was performed by the indigenous Jomon people as, by its very nature, *seppuku* requires the use of a sword and sword manufacture did not start in Japan until the second century BC. The first Japanese swords were copied from Chinese models, which were straight, long and unlike the slender, curved *tachi* and *katana* that would follow. Yet the Japanese did not only borrow the sword from China, but also grisly notions of what to do with it.

Many examples of suicide by the sword can be found in *The Annals of Lu Buwei*, a digest of Chinese history written in the third century BC. *The Annals of Lu Buwei* is crammed with accounts of suicide among the various members of its ruling class and those who served them. One such story is about two drinking companions who surmise they need look no further than each other as a source for food:

'You are meat and I am meat. Why should we seek meat elsewhere?' They thereupon soaked each other in sauce, then pulled out their knives and ate one another, stopping only when they had fallen over dead.[2]

The text also describes some of the first known accounts of stomach-cutting:

The Di army arrived and found Duke Yi at Rongze, where they killed him. They ate all his flesh, saving only his liver. When he arrived home Hong Yan reported on his mission … when he had finished, he cried out to Heaven and sobbed, stopping only after all the sadness had drained out from him. Then saying, 'Your servant requests that he serve as your outer garment,' he killed himself by cutting open his belly and putting Duke Yi's liver inside him.[3]

It did not take long for stomach-cutting to establish itself in Japan: by the twelfth century, the act of *seppuku* had become part of the national culture and, unlike China, it would spread beyond the domain of the nobility and into that of the martial elite. The first recorded accounts of *seppuku* occurred on the battlefield as a means of escape from likely enemy execution by decapitation or crucifixion. *Seppuku* in this instance also ensured that a warrior avoided any accusations of pusillanimity.

There was nothing cowardly, however, about the samurai archer and strongman Minamoto Tametomo. He was a twelfth-century commander fighting on the side of ex-emperor Sutoku during the Hōgen Rebellion (see page 56). But after Sutoku ignored Tametomo's suggested strategy of an attack on Emperor Go-Shirakawa's army, the rebellion failed. The victor's reprisals were brief and brutal – Minamoto rebels were executed by decapitation, including the dead body of a young Minamoto which was specially exhumed for this purpose. Tametomo was spared decapitation and, instead, sentenced to exile, after first having the sinews in his bow arm severed. However, this punishment would not prevent Tametomo from firing one last arrow against his Taira enemy some years later in northern Honshu. This particularly well-aimed and probably painful last shot would pass through two sides of a boatload of Taira samurai and sink it. In the end, though, the Taira trapped Tametomo in a house, where he would famously cut open his stomach while standing with his back against a pillar. While this gave Tametomo the dubious legacy of the first recorded *seppuku* suicide, more would occur in the Genpei War which followed.

BEHEADING AT THE BRIDGE

The Genpei War began when an aged Minamoto retainer called Yorimasa joined forces with a certain Prince Mochihito, who was trying to seize the throne. The first great battle of the war was fought in 1180 at the Uji Bridge. Yorimasa and Mochihito were trapped on one side of the river, as a handful of their warrior monks held back the Taira enemy from crossing. The monks not only displayed great heroism, but also committed *seppuku* when beaten. The *Heike Monogatari* described the scene:

> The soldier monks of Mii-dera with the Watanabe clan of Gensammi Nyudo's men vied with each other in pressing forward over the beams of the bridge, and fought till sundown, some returning with spoils, and some, after being wounded, cutting themselves open and jumping into the river.[4]

The Uji River was eventually forded by Taira horsemen and, with the day lost, Yorimasa prepared to face his final end. What followed was a famously celebrated episode in samurai history and introduces three elements into *seppuku*. The first is the writing of a death poem before the act, the second is the use of a retainer to behead a samurai in the throes of dying, and the third is the disposing of the head so it did not fall into enemy hands. The *Heike Monogatari* continued:

> Gensammi Nyudo [Yorimasa], calling Watanabe Choshichi Tanau, bade him strike off his head, but he refused, overcome by the thought of cutting off his master's head while alive, but offered to do so after he had committed suicide. Then Gensammi Nyudo, turning to the West, put his hands together and repeated the Nembutsu ten times in a loud voice, after which he composed this sad stanza: 'Like a fossil tree from which we gather-no-flowers sad has been my life, fated-no-fruit to produce.' And with these last words he thrust the point of his sword into his belly, and bowing his face to the ground pierced himself through and died. It was not a time when people usually make poems, but as he had been extremely fond of this pastime from his youth up, so even at the hour of

death he did not forget it. Choshichi Tonau took his head, and fastening stones to it sunk it in a deep part of the Ujigawa. Now though the Heike [Taira] samurai had been strictly ordered to take the Takiguchi Kiou alive, yet he, after fighting with great bravery, being very severely wounded, at last cut himself open and died.[5]

It would not be long before whole clans were committing *seppuku* after defeat in battle. A famous example of this occurred during Japan's medieval period at the city of Kamakura. Here, the Hōjō clan inherited power from the Minamoto and ruled Japan as regents for over a century. Trying to wrest control from the Hōjō was Emperor Go-Daigo, and the conflict culminated in the Battle of Kamakura in 1333, which was fought between the Hōjō defenders and the imperial army, led by Nitta Yoshisada. After a brief siege, Yoshisada's force broke through and stormed Kamakura, slaughtering its civilians and razing its buildings to the ground.

When the Hōjō realised they were overrun, they began the largest mass suicide in samurai history. The *Taiheiki* is a fourteenth-century record of the battle and describes the many acts of *seppuku* in graphic detail. This was something new for the Japanese annals, which previously recorded *seppuku* as an act performed by one or more warriors, but without being descriptive. Now, *seppuku* was not only limited to samurai but was also carried out by citizens. This abridged account focuses on the group *seppuku* led by the defending samurai, Nagasaki Takashige:

Now Nagasaki Takashige ran around to this place saying, 'Kill yourselves quickly! I shall go before you as your example!' ... and he cut his body with a long cut from left to right and fell down, pulling out his inwards ...Nagasaki Shin'uemon, a young boy fifteen years old that year, bowed before his grandfather, saying: 'Assuredly will the buddhas and gods give sanction to this deed. The filial descendant is he who brings honor to the name of his fathers.' With two thrusts of his dagger he slashed the veins of his aged grandfather's arms. He cut his own belly, pushed his grandfather down, and fell on top of him. Thereupon the Sagami lay monk also cut his belly, urged to duty by this youth newly come of age, and the castle lay monk did the same, while in the hall Hōjō kinsmen and men of other houses bared their snowy skins to the waist, some cutting open their bellies and some striking off their own heads. Truly two hundred and eighty-three men of the Hōjō took their lives, each striving to be first.[6]

The *Taiheiki* puts the number of deaths from Kamakura's mass *seppuku* at over 6,000, although it is difficult to substantiate this figure. Kamakura was certainly a chillingly unique event which was never to be repeated in such high numbers. However, news of the tragic deaths at Kamakura did not end the tradition of *seppuku* and, instead, it became an accepted part of society.

One particularly revered rationale for *seppuku* was its use as a display of devotion to a warrior's master. Since loyalty and self-sacrifice were two key elements of the samurai ethos, there was no greater way to honour a master than to die for him. The most celebrated example of a samurai's obedience until death was that of a fourteenth-century warrior, Kusunoki Masashige.

DEATH THROUGH FIDELITY

Masashige was a legendary Japanese warrior and the great exemplar of loyalty and self-sacrifice. Masashige immortalised himself when he was ordered by Go-Daigo to lead an army into an unwinnable battle. But, rather than refuse his master or even debate the matter, Masashige marched off devotedly to his death. In the end, Masashige, his brother and a handful of samurai retainers committed *seppuku* in an abandoned farmhouse. Before making the final cut, Masashige and his brother lamented not having seven more lives each to devote to the emperor.

The Battle of Kamakura also introduced the notion of *junshi*, or 'death through fidelity', to the act of *seppuku*. *Junshi* meant following one's master in death. This created another stage in a samurai's loyalty, by allowing them to serve their master beyond the grave. An often repeated example of *junshi* is the story of Tomoe Gozen, also made famous for being a female samurai. Gozen was one of a handful of retainers to continue protecting Genpei War commander Yoshinaka in his last hour. Gozen pleaded to be allowed to die fighting for Yoshinaka, but he ordered her to escape from the field of battle, which she did, killing dozens of enemy samurai in the process. Upon hearing of Yoshinaka's death, however, Gozen simply jumped into the sea and drowned herself.

As the medieval period of Japan wore on, *junshi* became not just an occasional occurrence but a ubiquitous feature of samurai society. It is celebrated most famously in the story of the 47 *Rōnin*.

THE 47 RŌNIN

In 1701 Asano Naganori, *daimyo* – or ruler – of the Ako clan, was visiting Edo Castle with some other dignitaries. But Naganori had not brought an expensive enough present for Kira Yoshinaka, the Master of Ceremonies, who, if properly bribed, would ensure proceedings in the castle went smoothly. Offended by Naganori's miserly gift, Yoshinaka began insulting him by making faces and mocking the way he spoke. After a while Naganori could bear it no more and attacked Yoshinaka with a dagger. Although Yoshinaka came away with only a small injury to his face, the *shōgun* ruled that court officials should not be harmed in the castle, and commanded Naganori to commit *seppuku*.

This left forty-seven of Naganori's men without a master, making all of them *rōnin* and honour-bound to avenge their *daimyo*'s death. Anticipating a reprisal, however, Yoshinaka had his spies put the *rōnin* under surveillance. The *rōnin* leader. Ōishi Yoshio, disbanded the group and moved to Kyoto, where he started drinking, visiting geisha houses and generally behaving most unlike a samurai. At one point in the story, Yoshio had passed out drunk in a gutter and was spat on by a passer-by, disgusted that a samurai would act in such a way.

After a year, Yoshinaka's spies brought him news of Yoshio's drunken and debauched behaviour, so Yoshinaka considered himself safe and called off his men. Then, one snowy night, a year and a half after the death of Naganori, the forty-seven *rōnin* made their attack on Yoshinaka's mansion. They broke into two groups, crept quietly inside, killed all who opposed them and found Yoshinaka, identifying him by the scar Naganori had given him with his dagger. Yoshio gave Yoshinaka the chance to commit *seppuku*, and even offered to be his second, but Yoshinaka could not go through with it. So Yoshio beheaded him and placed his head on Naganori's grave. All of the *rōnin* handed themselves over to the *shōgun*.

This presented the *shōgun* with a dilemma: on one hand the *rōnin* had acted honourably according to the *bushidō* code; on the other, they had defied the *shōgun*'s order that there was to be no retaliation for Naganori's death. He therefore decided all of the *rōnin* responsible should be put to death, but they would be allowed to carry it out themselves by committing *seppuku*. The *rōnin* committed group suicide by Naganori's grave and were subsequently buried around him, the site becoming a shrine for pilgrims to visit and celebrate the honourable *rōnin*. Legend has it that one such pilgrim was the man who had spat on Yoshio in the street. After crying by Yoshio's grave and begging for forgiveness, the man also committed *seppuku*.

Some accounts of the *47 Rōnin* report that many of the *rōnin*'s wives committed *seppuku* in honour of their dead husbands. This female equivalent of *seppuku* was called *jigai*, and was carried out by first tying the legs together so as to die in a dignified pose, before cutting open the jugular.

THE EDO PERIOD

During the relatively peaceful Edo Period, there were fewer chances for a samurai to commit *seppuku* in battle or to follow his fallen master through *junshi*. Nevertheless, *seppuku* continued to thrive and *junshi* was still carried out by a samurai whose master had died of natural causes. But there was another reason for the continued rise of *seppuku* – its use as a capital punishment. Using *seppuku* to execute people was not a new idea: *Shōgun* Tokugawa Ieyasu had famously invited his detractors to commit *seppuku* after their defeat at the Battle of Sekigahara in 1600. The battle represented one of the last fought by the samurai and, with warfare occurring less often, large numbers of newly unemployed samurai were causing trouble. *Seppuku* as capital punishment acted as a stiff incentive for them to behave.

The typical offences committed by samurai would today probably be classified as misdemeanours rather than serious crimes. They included petty theft, embezzlement, womanising, insulting a lord and habouring Christians. The penalty remained the same for all – death by *seppuku*. Predictably, the samurai offence which occurred most often was fighting. For a samurai to indulge in common scraps and bar brawls was considered unacceptable, and in the mid-sixteenth century a law had been passed to prosecute anyone involved. The law was called *kenka ryoseihai*, and it ended up meaning both parties in a dispute would be punished equally, regardless of the nature of the dispute and who was responsible for causing it. During Tokugawa Ieyasu's reign as *shōgun* in the early seventeenth century, *kenka ryoseihai* was treated more as a guideline than a rule, but instances of execution by *seppuku* rose exponentially nonetheless.

Seppuku during the Edo Period was not always a result of wandering samurai indulging in petty brawling, as the period also included uprisings, rebellions and assassination attempts. There was no more serious crime than trying to kill a high-ranking samurai or a member of the royal line, and when this occurred no quarter was given, even for the very young. Instead, it was considered lenient to allow the perpetrators the chance to die honourably. The following example is described in Inazō Nitobe's text on *bushidō*:

> Two brothers, Sakon and Naiki, respectively twenty-four and seventeen years of age, made an effort to kill Iyéyasu in order to avenge their father's wrongs; but before they could enter the camp they were made prisoners. The old general admired the pluck of the youths who dared an attempt on his life and ordered that they should be allowed to die an honorable death. Their little brother Hachimaro, a mere infant of eight summers, was condemned to a similar fate, as the sentence was pronounced on all the

male members of the family, and the three were taken to a monastery where it was to be executed. A physician who was present on the occasion has left us a diary from which the following scene is translated. 'When they were all seated in a row for final dispatch, Sakon turned to the youngest and said – 'Go thou first, for I wish to be sure that thou doest it aright.' Upon the little one's replying that, as he had never seen seppuku performed, he would like to see his brothers do it and then he could follow them, the older brothers smiled between their tears: 'Well said, little fellow! So canst thou well boast of being our father's child.' When they had placed him between them, Sakon thrust the dagger into the left side of his own abdomen and asked, 'Look, brother! Doest understand now? Only, don't push the dagger too far, lest thou fall back. Lean forward, rather, and keep thy knees well composed.' Naiki did likewise and said to the boy, 'Keep thine eyes open or else thou mayst look like a dying woman. If thy dagger feels anything within and thy strength fails, take courage and double thy effort to cut across.' The child looked from one to the other, and when both had expired, he calmly half denuded himself and followed the example set him on either hand.[7]

As a result of the rise in *seppuku* as capital punishment during the Edo Period, more attention was paid to its ceremonial aspects. From the seventeenth century, many texts were published on *bushidō* and *seppuku*, as now there was less to keep the samurai occupied and more time to explain how they should behave. Some of these codes and manuals also gave detailed instruction on the procedure of the *seppuku* ceremony. The following is a composite of the protocol of a *seppuku* ceremony based on A.B. Mitford's *Old Tales of Japan*:

THE SEPPUKU CEREMONY

The Location
In modern times the ceremony has taken place either in the palace or in the garden of a daimyo, to whom the condemned man has been given in charge. Whether it takes place in the palace or in the garden depends upon the rank of the individual.

Preparing the Site

If the execution takes place in a room, white cotton cloth should be laid down and mats prepared. Two red rugs should be spread over all; for if the white cotton cloth be used alone the blood will soak through on to the mats. If the execution be at night candlesticks should be placed lest the seconds be hindered in their work, but an excessive illumination is not decorous. Two screens covered with white paper should be set up to conceal the dirk [*wakizashi* sword] upon a tray, a bucket to hold the head after it has been cut off, an incense burner, a pail of water, and a basin.

The above rules apply equally when *hara-kiri* takes place in a garden. In the latter case the place is hung round with a white curtain. When the ceremony takes place in the garden, matting must be spread all the way to the place, so that sandals need not be worn. The reason for this is that some men in that position suffer from a rush of blood to the head from nervousness, so their sandals might slip off their feet without their being aware of their loss and as this would have a very bad appearance.

The Principal

The retainers of the palace going to the room where the prisoner is confined inform him that, as the censors have arrived, he should change his dress. The attendants bring out a change of clothes upon a large tray: it is when he has finished his toilet that the witnesses go forth and take their places and the principal is then introduced.

Censors

When a man has been ordered by the Government to disembowel himself, the public censors who have been appointed to act as witnesses proceed to the place of execution, dressed in their hempen-cloth dress of ceremony. The chief censor then announces to the lord of the palace that he has come to read out the sentence of the condemned. Tea and sweetmeats are set before the censors, but they decline to accept any hospitality until their business has been concluded.

The Sentence

The chief censor should take his place in front of the criminal at a distance of twelve feet. He must read out the sentence distinctly. If the sentence be a long document, to begin reading in a very loud voice and afterwards drop into a whisper has an appearance of faint-heartedness; but to read it throughout in a low voice is worse still: it should be delivered clearly from beginning to end. When the sentence has been read, it is probable that the condemned man will have some last words to say. It must depend on the nature of what he has to say whether it will be received or not. If he speaks in a confused or bewildered manner no attention is paid to it: his second should lead him away, of his own accord or at a sign from the chief witness.

The condemned man should answer in the following way: 'Sirs, I thank you for your careful consideration, but I have nothing that I wish to say. I am greatly indebted to you for the great kindness which I have received since I have been under your charge. I beg you to take my respects to your lord and to the gentlemen of your clan who have treated me so well.' Or he may say, 'Sirs, I have nothing to say. Yet, since you are so kind as to think of me, I should be obliged if you would deliver such and such a message to such a one.' This is the proper and becoming sort of speech for the occasion.

Seconds

For seconds, men are wanted who have distinguished themselves in the military arts. Every samurai should be able to cut off a man's head: therefore, to have to employ a stranger to act as second is to incur the charge of ignorance of the arts of war, and is a bitter mortification. These seconds attend upon the condemned man when he changes his dress and sit by him whilst the sentence is being read. They must understand that should there be any mistake they must throw the condemned man, and, holding him down, cut off his head or stab him to death.

When the execution is carried out with proper solemnity, three men are employed. Their duties are as follows: the chief second [*kaishaku*] strikes off the head; he is the most important officer in the execution by *hara-kiri*. The assistant second brings forward the tray on which is placed the dirk.

This should be produced very quietly when the principal takes his place. The third second carries the head to the chief witness for identification.

The *Kaishaku*

When a man is appointed to act as second to another, what shall be said of him if he accepts the office with a smiling face? Yet must he not put on a face of distress. To play the coward and yield up the office to another man is out of the question. When a man is called upon to perform the office, he should express his readiness to borrow his principal's sword in some such terms as the following: 'As I am to have the honour of being your second, I would fain borrow your sword for the occasion. It may be a consolation to you to perish by your own sword, with which you are familiar.' If, however, the principal declines and prefers to be executed with the second's sword, his wish must be complied with. If the second should make an awkward cut with his own sword it is a disgrace to him; therefore he should borrow someone else's sword, so that the blame may rest with the sword and not with the swordsman.

The Act

The condemned man should be caused to die as quickly as possible. Should he wish for some water to drink, it should be given to him. If in his talk he should express himself like a noble samurai, all pains should be exhausted in carrying out his execution. Yet however careful a man he may be, as he nears his death his usual demeanour will undergo a change. If the execution is delayed, in all probability it will cause the prisoner's courage to fail him; therefore, as soon as the sentence shall have been passed, the execution should be brought to a conclusion.

The principal should sit facing the west, the second facing the north. When the principal has taken his place, the second strips his right shoulder of the dress of ceremony, which he allows to fall behind his sleeve. Then the assistant second brings out the tray on which is laid the dirk. The principal reaches out his hand to draw the tray towards him. He then inserts the dirk in the left side of his belly and drags it to the right.

Decapitation

There are three rules for the time of cutting off the head: the first is when the dirk is laid on the tray; the second is when the principal looks at the left side of his belly before inserting the dirk; the third is when he inserts the dirk. Then the blow should be struck without delay. If he has struck off the head at a blow without failure, the second should retire backward a little and wipe his weapon kneeling; he should have plenty of white paper ready in his bosom to wipe away the blood and rub up his sword. Having replaced his sword in its scabbard, he should readjust his upper garments and take his seat to the rear. In the event of the second making a false cut, so as not to strike off the head at a blow, the second must take the head by the top-knot, and, pressing it down, cut it off. Should he take bad aim and cut the shoulder by mistake, and should the principal rise and cry out, before he has time to writhe, he should hold him down and stab him to death, and then cut off his head, or the assistant seconds, who are sitting behind, should come forward and hold him down, while the chief second cuts off his head. If the body does not fall at once, which is said to be sometimes the case, the second should pull the feet to make it fall.

There are some who say that the perfect way to cut off the head is not to cut right through the neck at a blow, but to leave a little uncut, and, as the head hangs by the skin, to seize the top-knot and slice it off. After the head is cut off, the eyes are apt to blink and the mouth to move and to bite the pebbles and sand. This being hateful to see, at what amongst samurai is so important an occasion, and being a shameful thing, it is held to be best not to let the head fall, but to hold back a little in delivering the blow. Yet it is a very difficult matter to cut so as to leave the head hanging by a little flesh, and there is the danger of missing the cut; and as any mistake in the cut is most horrible to see it is better to strike a fair blow at once.

The Head

When the head has fallen, the junior second should enter, and, taking up the head, present it to the witness for inspection. He should take the head in his right hand, holding it by the top-knot of hair and advance towards the witness, passing on the right side of the corpse, resting the chin of the head upon the hilt of his sword, and kneeling on his left knee to show the profile of the head. It is also laid down as another rule that the second, laying down his sword, should take out paper from the bosom of his dress, and placing the head in the palm of his left hand, and taking the top-knot of hair in his right hand, should lay the head upon the paper, and so submit it for inspection. If the head be bald, he should pierce the left ear with the stiletto carried in the scabbard of his dirk, and so carry it to be identified. He must carry thick paper in the bosom of his dress. Inside the paper he shall place a bag with rice bran and ashes, in order that he may carry the head without being sullied by the blood. When the identification of the head is concluded, the junior second's duty is to place it in a bucket and the ceremony is concluded.[8]

AN EYEWITNESS ACCOUNT

The ceremony of *seppuku* had reached its zenith at the time Japan opened her doors to outsiders in the mid-nineteenth century. After more than 200 years without foreign influence, the act of *seppuku* and its ritual ceremony provided a horrifying spectacle for visiting dignitaries. One such man was Algernon Bertram Freeman-Mitford, a British lord and diplomat working for the foreign office during the Meiji Restoration. Mitford had the rare honour of observing a *seppuku* ceremony in 1868, only a few years before the samurai class was abolished altogether. From then on, *seppuku*'s place as samurai ritual would cease to exist, although the act would continue as a national phenomenon into the twentieth century. The most striking examples of *seppuku* in the modern age were performed by officers during the Japanese defeat at the end of the Second World War. The conflict is also notable for the country's mass production of samurai swords, some of which were placed inside the cockpits of *kamikaze* pilots about to commit another form of martial suicide.

Mitford's description of the *seppuku* ceremony in his 1871 book, *Tales of Old Japan*, is one of the few eyewitness accounts, and certainly the only one written in English. It gives a fascinating insight into the samurai tradition, which lived on after the warrior class had officially ended:

I may here describe an instance of such an execution which I was sent officially to witness. The condemned man was Taki Zenzaburō, an officer of the Prince of Bizen, who gave the order to fire upon the foreign settlement at Hiogo in the month of February 1868 ... The ceremony, which was ordered by the Mikado himself, took place at 10.30 at night in the temple of Seifukuji ... We were invited to follow the Japanese witnesses into the hondo or main hall of the temple, where the ceremony was to be performed. It was an imposing scene. A large hall with a high roof supported by dark pillars of wood. From the ceiling hung a profusion of those huge gilt lamps and ornaments peculiar to Buddhist temples. In front of the high altar, where the floor, covered with beautiful white mats, is raised some three or four inches from the ground, was laid a rug of scarlet felt. Tall candles placed at regular intervals gave out a dim mysterious light, just sufficient to let all the proceedings be seen. The seven Japanese took their places on the left of the raised floor, the seven foreigners on the right. No other person was present.

After an interval of a few minutes of anxious suspense, Taki Zenzaburō, a stalwart man, thirty-two years of age, with a noble air, walked into the hall attired in his dress of ceremony, with the peculiar hempen-cloth wings which are worn on great occasions. He was accompanied by a kaishaku and three officers, who wore the jimbaori or war surcoat with gold-tissue facings. With the kaishaku on his left hand, Taki Zenzaburō advanced slowly towards the Japanese witnesses, and the two bowed before them, then drawing near to the foreigners they saluted us in the same way, perhaps even with more deference: in each case the salutation was ceremoniously returned.

Slowly, and with great dignity, the condemned man mounted on to the raised floor, prostrated himself before the high altar twice, and seated himself on the felt carpet with his back to the high altar, the kaishaku crouching on his left-hand side. One of the three attendant officers then came forward, bearing a stand of the kind used in temples for offerings, on which, wrapped in paper, lay the wakizashi, the short sword or dirk of the Japanese, nine inches and a half in length, with a point and an edge as sharp as a razor's. This he handed, prostrating himself, to the condemned man, who received it reverently, raising it to his head with both hands, and placed it in front of himself.

After another profound obeisance, Taki Zenzaburō, in a voice which betrayed just so much emotion and hesitation as might be expected from a man who is making a painful confession, but with no sign of either in his face or manner, spoke as follows: 'I, and I alone, unwarrantably gave the order to fire on the foreigners at Kôbé, and again as they tried to escape. For this crime I disembowel myself, and I beg you who are present to do me the honour of witnessing the act.'

Bowing once more, the speaker allowed his upper garments to slip down to his girdle, and remained naked to the waist. Carefully, according to custom, he tucked his sleeves under his knees to prevent himself from falling backwards; for a noble Japanese gentleman should die falling forwards. Deliberately, with a steady hand, he took the dirk that lay before him; he looked at it wistfully, almost affectionately; for a moment he seemed to collect his thoughts for the last time, and then stabbing himself deeply below the waist on the left-hand side, he drew the dirk slowly across to the right side, and, turning it in the wound, gave a slight cut upwards. During this sickeningly painful operation he never moved a muscle of his face. When he drew out the dirk, he leaned forward and stretched out his neck; an expression of pain for the first time crossed his face, but he uttered no sound. At that moment the kaishaku, who, still crouching by his side, had been keenly watching his every movement, sprang to his feet, poised his sword for a second in the air; there was a flash, a heavy, ugly thud, a crashing fall; with one blow the head had been severed from the body.

A dead silence followed, broken only by the hideous noise of the blood throbbing out of the inert heap before us, which but a moment before had been a brave and chivalrous man. It was horrible. The kaishaku made a low bow, wiped his sword with a piece of paper which he had ready for the purpose, and retired from the raised floor; and the stained dirk was solemnly borne away, a bloody proof of the execution.

The two representatives of the Mikado then left their places, and, crossing over to where the foreign witnesses sat, called us to witness that the sentence of death upon Taki Zenzaburō had been faithfully carried out. The ceremony being at an end, we left the temple.[9]

NOTES

1   *The Field of Honor*, Benjamin C. Truman, 1884.

2   *The Annals of Lu Buwei*, translated by John Knoblock and Jeffrey Riegel

3   Ibid.

4   *Heike Monogatari*, translated by A.L. Sadler, 1918

5   Ibid.

6   *Taiheiki: A Chronicle of Medieval Japan*, translated by Helen Craig McCullough, 1959

7   *Bushidō: The Soul of Japan*, Inazō Nitobe, 1900

8   *Records of Suicide by Sword*, Kudo Yukihiro, translated by A.B. Mitford, 1871

9   *Tales of Old Japan*, A.B. Mitford, 1871

3

The Heian Period

BEGINNINGS AND BORDERS

The history of the samurai is inseparable from Japan's landscape, which is a crescent-shaped archipelago of 6,852 islands. Japan's closest neighbour is Korea and the two are separated by the Sea of Japan – a treacherous stretch of water which has a deadly legacy of typhoons, storms and shipwrecks. This made a sea voyage to Japan a hazardous and potentially fatal endeavour, ensuring the country was left in seclusion from the rest of the world for many centuries of its early history.

However, Japan's story is not one of complete isolation, as much was borrowed from Korea and China – political systems, agricultural knowledge, written language, architecture, various technologies, religion and military conscription. It is fair to say, though, that every foreign object, theme and idea was adapted into the unique Japanese culture, and these adaptations mostly took place away from the eyes of the world. Any foreign influences considered disruptive or unhelpful were expelled and Japan's borders closed. Japan lived for over 200 years in self-imposed exile, where its leaders had complete authority to create an identity and culture that was safe from alien agendas. But the world would not allow Japan to be left alone forever, and in 1853 American gunboats ordered Japan to reopen its doors for foreign business.

Ten thousand years ago there was no need for a boat to cross into what is now modern-day Japan. Then, the country was simply connected to mainland Asia. But with the end of the last ice age came a global glacial melt and the seas rose to encircle Japan's islands. Emerging among thousands of smaller counterparts were the large main islands of Kyūshū, Shikoku, Honshu and Hokkaido.

The islands' original inhabitants were the Jomon people, best known for inventing the first clay pots, which incorporated a coiled rope style. The Jomon represented a shift in hunter-gatherer trends worldwide – that is, they opted to stay put. For the Jomon, this meant occupying caves around the coastal regions of the Japanese islands and consuming a diet consisting mainly of fish. It would be some centuries before the Jomon descendants, the Ainu, and later arrivals, the Yayoi, developed serious forms of agriculture such as rice farming. The reason for this is that 80 per cent of Japan is covered with mountains and there are few plains; in fact, the total amount of arable land during the samurai period was less than 15 per cent.

The majority of the flat land in samurai times was concentrated into three important geographical points on Honshu Island – the Nobi, Kinai and Kanto plains. The history of the samurai is largely concerned with the continual struggle for control of these areas, especially the Kinai plain where the early imperial capital cities were based. Around the top of the Kinai plain is Lake Biwa, which splits Honshu in two. To the south-west of Honshu are the islands of Shikoku and Kyūshū, with the latter the closest point to Korea on the Asian mainland. As such, Kyūshū was often the landing and leaving point for invaders and attackers respectively. To the north-east of the Kinai plain lies a barrier of high mountains, which in the pre-samurai age were considered outlying barbarian badlands beyond the emperor's control. The inhabitants of this rugged countryside were the Emishi, an indigenous tribal race who were descended from the Jomon and Ainu.

The Emishi were considered backward by the Japanese – they spoke a different language, wore tattoos and were curiously hairy. The imperial court felt duty-bound to 'civilise' the Emishi as part of their policy of land expansion in the area. This began the Emishi's dubious legacy of being colonised by the Japanese, and, as with other indigenous cultures placed in similar circumstances, the Emishi responded variously to their oppressors. Some Emishi tribes were hospitable and welcomed their new sword-carrying visitors, others eyed the new military outposts suspiciously before giving a gradual acceptance. Many Emishi were simply bewildered by the imperial 'gifts' such as flags and drums. Whatever the initial impressions, it soon became obvious that the settlers from the south not only intended to stay permanently, but also expected tax and tributes from their hirsute subjects.

ALLIES AND ENEMIES

To the Japanese, the Emishi were defined in two ways: allies of the court (*fushu* and *ifu*), and those who were hostile (*iteki*). Predictably, after systems of tax were imposed, many Emishi became more *iteki* than *fushu* or *ifu*, but there was certainly no united Emishi policy of aggression against the Japanese, and each tribe adopted its own rules. Japanese generals were, therefore, often astonished to find that a peace deal brokered with Emishi in one valley was not recognised in the next. Hostile Emishi tribes were not interested in Japanese ideas of civilisation, which had been largely borrowed from China, and Japanese methods of warfare, also based on the Chinese military model, were even less relevant. An arranged battle on an open plain between two facing armies of spear-carrying infantrymen was meaningless to mounted Emishi warriors used to fighting at close quarters in dense forests and narrow mountain passes. Theirs was a brutally efficient form of guerrilla warfare fought with bow, arrow and sword. As a result, the Japanese army often found itself fighting a difficult foe.

Japanese troops, mainly conscripted peasants, seemed unsuited for Emishi warfare, and they were also unwilling and uninterested in adapting their methods. To make up for their army's ineptitude, Japanese generals sent back reports of whole Emishi tribes surrendering to them – which in reality meant that no resistance had been met. At other times, however, there was no way of stopping the embarrassing truth reaching imperial ears. At the Battle of Subuse in 788, over 1,200 troops were killed in a blundering defeat against the Emishi, even through they outnumbered them six to one.

These battlefield humiliations infuriated Emperor Kammu, but there was also an impression that the skirmishes on the far northern frontiers were of little relevance to the peaceful and civilised south. After a while, Kammu decided there was no need for an army to protect the imperial capital of Nara, and as the army in the north appeared to be worse than useless, he disbanded that too. In the end, Kammu decided to abandon the Chinese model of military conscription altogether. Instead, the army would be replaced by the provincial clans who would continue the war against the Emishi on the emperor's behalf.

As well as cutting the cost of paying an ineffectual national army, any conflicts would remain contained to the northern areas between the Emishi barbarians and the fighters who lived there. This freed up funds for Kammu to uproot his capital in Nara and move it to the city of Heian-kyō. The new site, which became commonly known as Kyoto, would remain the capital for 1,000 years, and the years 794–1185 are known as the Heian Period. Ultimately, while farming out his military problems must have seemed like an ideal solution to the reigning emperor, it would have far-reaching consequences for the imperial powerbase in the centuries to come.

The rugged terrain of the northern wilderness was no place for military amateurs and, instead, it became a proving ground for fledgling warriors to learn their skills in battle with the Emishi. The only way to defeat them was to learn their style of warfare, and it soon became common for the Japanese clans charged with guarding and protecting the northern frontiers to include *fushu* and *ifu* Emishi warriors in their ranks. The mainstay of the Emishi fighting force was the mounted archer, who held his bow at the lower end to maintain balance on horseback while firing. Emishi bows were fired at alarmingly close range, forcing the rider to draw across his left-hand side and turn in tight anti-clockwise circles around his target to maintain an attack. When a warrior was compelled to abandon his bow, he could continue fighting with his sword, the long blade of which was shaped with a deliberate curve to enable a slashing action. It was not long before the Japanese were updating their straight Chinese model of sword with a curved blade to emulate the Emishi style. To go with the new swords, warriors designed a lighter form of armour made of leather strips that enabled a mounted archer freedom of movement. It is ironic that the military traditions of the 'barbaric' Emishi, evolved and perfected over centuries of battling on Japanese terrain, would form the basis of the fighting techniques employed by the Japanese martial elite that followed – the samurai.

CLANS OF THE COURT

While life in the far north of Honshu included sporadic attacks by Emishi and various bandits, those in the centre of the island did not look far beyond the gates of the new capital, Kyoto. It was considered the cultural hub of the civilised world, and most courtiers and nobles found it unthinkable that there could be a worthwhile life outside it.

However, many nobles without a legitimate purpose in the capital were forced to live in the provinces, and the imperial court was becoming overrun with its own blue blood. For centuries, the most influential clan at court had been the Fujiwara, mainly because every emperor wanted to marry one of its beautiful daughters. As a result, after Kammu, the imperial family grew exponentially: Kammu's grandson, Saga, alone sired forty-nine children by nine empresses during his twenty-four-year reign (809–23). There was a limit to how many extra mouths the imperial coffers could afford to feed, let alone the growing numbers of leisurely aristocrats roaming the capital city. Since there was a limited number of official imperial positions, many nobles decided to seek their fortunes in the provinces after all. The rest were simply told to leave. Saga himself decided that thirty of his sons would be sent to the countryside, albeit furnished with new surnames. Many of these nobles would be called Minamoto, and others would become Taira.

The provinces were soon replete with dispossessed nobles and aristocrats, and after a time they became wealthy landowners and heads of powerful clans. Beneath the landowners were farmers and small-holders, who paid them rent and dividends. Later, the relationship became more than financial – bonds were formed, often through inter-marriage, and a quasi-feudal structure was created. At the top was the 'master' landowner, usually of royal lineage, and underneath him was the 'samurai', or 'one who serves'. The word samurai did not originally have a military meaning, but it was expected that in times of trouble the samurai would take up arms to protect their master. And because the clans lived along the perilous frontier borders, violent attack was an ever-present threat. So the farmers became skilled with weapons and, after a few generations, matured into hardened warriors. These warriors would then be used to keep the borders safe in the name of the emperor.

Skirmishes with the Emishi kept the warriors in fighting form, and it was natural that the clans that prospered were those at the farthest and most dangerous reaches of the empire. Here they were left to develop their military skills away from the imperial gaze or interference from rival clans. By the tenth century, the definition of samurai had changed, referring now to a clan's fighting elite – a warrior order prepared to fight to the death at their master's command. The age of the samurai had begun.

FOUR POWERBASES

By the eleventh century, three powerful clans had become prominent in Japan – the Fujiwara, the Minamoto and the Taira. The Fujiwara, as we have seen, had cemented its position as the leading family of the court through marriage since the seventh century. The clan further consolidated its imperial powerbase by developing its own army after the court's move to Kyoto, and continued to dominate Japanese politics up until the twelfth century by controlling the succession to the throne and occupying most of the government and administrative posts. While the Fujiwara held a monopoly at court, however, the rising stars of the provinces were the Minamoto and the Taira.

The Taira would first establish themselves in the western plains of Kanto, where they forged a reputation as a cultured and civilised clan that brought style and refinement to an otherwise coarse and uncouth provincial world. The Taira thought so highly of themselves that Taira Masakado, a blood relative of Kammu, began calling himself the 'new emperor' in 939, in direct opposition to the ruling emperor. His rebellion was quelled, but the Taira's haughtiness and ambition would continue for many centuries.

If the Taira could sum up all the vulgarities of the provinces in one name, it would have undoubtedly chosen the Minamoto, who had a reputation for being hairy, unkempt and rough. After leaving the capital, the Minamoto would set themselves up on the Kanto plains in the far east of the empire, where fighting against the Emishi was a persistent problem. The rapid expansion of these clans meant that it would not be long before the two opposing sides of the samurai culture would be fighting for control over the empire.

In addition to the three samurai clans, there was a fourth, unlikely military power – the warrior monks. Buddhism had spread from Korea to Japan in the sixth century, when Crown Prince Shotoku combined the foreign religion with traditional Shintō beliefs. In the early seventh century, three great Buddhist temples were built in the then capital city, Nara, namely Hōryū-ji, Yakushu-ji and the spectacular Tōdai-ji, or 'Great Eastern Temple'. Tōdai-ji's glory would be a 50ft bronze and gold Buddha, which weighed over 550 tons – a statue whose manufacture seriously depleted the country's copper reserves. At the unveiling, the then emperor, Shōmu, proclaimed himself the servant of three things – Buddha, the law and the priesthood.

This claim did not escape the priests, who began accumulating enough money and power to rival the imperial court itself. To do so, the priesthood made itself exempt from most forms of land tax. Taxes, the priests felt, were not suitable for an organisation charged with keeping the empire free of starvation, sickness and spiritual strife. The monks, many of whom had benefited from a Chinese education, spent their tax-free money in developing tracts of unused land, which would then provide substantial profits when sold.

By the eighth century, the Nara temples enjoyed real influence at the imperial court. This created an uneasy tension between the two institutions, which reached breaking point over a scandal involving an empress and a Buddhist priest. The emperor managed to avoid direct confrontation with the priesthood by moving the capital to Kyoto, but the affair had exposed a moral squalor within the temple and many were shocked.

One priest, a monk called Saichō, was so disgusted by his Nara counterparts that he set up his own temple. Saichō built this temple, Enryaku-ji, on Mount Hiei by Lake Biwa and devoted it to purely spiritual concerns. It soon became the official guardian temple for the new capital at Kyoto. Enryaku-ji was joined by a sister temple, Mii-dera, and it was not long before both monasteries were imperial favourites. As the temples of Kyoto grew rich and powerful, so did the feelings of resentment at Nara, and a violent rivalry developed between the Kyoto and Nara priests.

PRIESTLY ARMS RACE

Arms and fighting men became commonplace in all Buddhist temples from the end of the tenth century. It was no secret that the priestly coffers were full to bursting and, at a time of inter-clan conflict, political instability and zealous government taxation, the priests moved to protect their wealth. It was not long before each temple had its own private army.

For the next 200 years the main temples of Nara and Kyoto had enough military power to rival the imperial court, and they were quick to use it against any imperial 'interference'. The outside appointment of clergy members, for example, caused particular resentment among the priests, but the temples, as well as controlling large armies, also had religion on their side. An army of angry priests marching into Kyoto brought not only weapons but the fury of the gods, and the priests would play on the fears of the people by carrying a wooden shrine called a *mikoshi* on their shoulders. The *mikoshi* was believed to house the deity it represented, so attacking or damaging it was sacrilege. The practice of leaving a *mikoshi* in the middle of a city street would usually be enough to frighten citizens and courtiers into letting the priests have their way.

While the temples made it clear they would not take orders from the court, they usually reserved any actual military action for each other. The priestly armies developed something of an arms race, which resulted in some rather suspect recruiting processes. Warrior monks, known as *sōhei*, were at this time often mercenaries, criminals or peasants without any obvious priestly attributes apart from a shaven head. They typically wore a long white robe over leather plate armour, wooden clogs or straw sandals, and a white headcowl covering most of their head. The *sōhei*'s main weapon was the *naginata*.

Conflict between the temples was almost never waged on religious grounds, as there was general consensus on matters of doctrine. Instead, disputes arose over land ownership or points of honour, and by the eleventh century loyalties based on geographical location were abandoned. The Nara temples – Hōryū-ji, Yakushu-ji and Tōdai-ji – were just as likely to attack one another as their greatest rivals – Enryaku-ji and Mii-dera – in Kyoto. The same policy applied to Enryaku-ji and Mii-dera. In 1080, for example, the Ōmi people, under the protection of the Enryaku-ji, attacked the Otsu, who were protected by the Mii-dera temple. The Enryaku-ji showed little concern about the Otsu, so the Otsu instead went to the Mii-dera, who suggested the Otsu's best form of action was to end their relationship with the Enryaku-ji. This advice did not sit well with the Enryaku-ji priests themselves and, in response, they sent an army to burn Mii-dera to the ground – the first of four occasions in the eleventh century that Enryaku-ji *sōhei* razed Mii-dera. Mii-dera's retaliation was quick but short lived. Instead, a rumour emerged that both sides had reconciled their differences and now planned a joint attack on the imperial capital.

The threat of a priestly attack filled the court with an overwhelming sense of dread. Kyoto could not withstand any assault from two armies, especially those composed of bloodthirsty warrior monks. To protect the capital, the emperor turned to the greatest samurai warlord of the time – Minamoto Yoshiie (see page 126). Yoshiie reinforced the city's defences and armed it with a garrison of his finest warriors. In the end there was no attack, but the emperor's actions had some unintended consequences that were not lost on the priests or the samurai. He had shown that his own imperial guard could not protect the capital against an aggressor, and he would need outside help. This was tantamount to admitting that the provincial samurai clans were now the top military power in the country.

The dispossessed princes and nobles once exiled from the capital to the frontier were now back as formidable clan warlords. And now, as well as being protectors of the empire, these clans would exert power over it. As a result, with three clans – Fujiwara, Taira and Minamoto – all vying for leadership, much blood was going to be spilt.

THE HŌGEN REBELLION

Surprisingly, when the first clash came, the clans did not divide along family lines. Instead, the Hōgen Rebellion was a far more elaborate and entangled episode, which played out according to the perplexing laws of civil war. The end of the rebellion would allow the rise of the first samurai-led government in Japanese history.

The Hōgen Rebellion began when the emperor abdicated in favour of his son. This was a common system among medieval Japanese emperors. The young emperor would perform all of the necessary ceremonial duties, while the ex-emperor would retain actual control, usually pulling the strings from the monastery where he had 'retired'. This was called the Insei system, or cloistered rule. The system was designed to stabilise the emperorship by keeping it within one bloodline, but in the Hōgen Rebellion it actually pitted the ex-emperor against the officially reigning emperor.

Emperor Toba had abdicated in 1123, but continued to rule using the Insei system over his son, Sutoku. He then forced Sutoku to retire and installed Sutoku's brother, Konoe, on the throne. So in 1150, there was one emperor and two ex-emperors. However, Konoe was a sickly child and died as teenager, and while Sutoku expressed his interest in ruling again, Toba instead crowned another son, Go-Shirakawa. Courtiers then persuaded Sutoku to reclaim his birthright by force. The most vocal of these plotters was Fujiwara Yorinaga, Imperial Minister of the Right – the highest office of government, second only to the regent. Yorinaga told Sutoku that he would find armed support, not just from the Fujiwara at court, but among the warrior monks of Nara and the samurai clans of the provinces. The idea had an irresistible appeal to Sutoku, who was more than ten years older than his sibling. The path became clearer when ex-emperor Toba succumbed to a long illness and died in 1156.

Go-Shirakawa may have been the younger brother and did not have Sutoku's friends at court, but he was still emperor and far from stupid. As Sutoku sent out word to summon support from the provincial samurai and the Nara monks, Go-Shirakawa did the same with his potential supporters. The samurai forces that heralded these summons would be divided, not along clan lines but by previous alliances. Consequently, a complicated mixture of Taira, Minamoto and Fujiwara samurai would fight for both Go-Shirakawa and Sutoku. Leading the Taira for the Sutoku side was Tadamasa, the uncle of Kiyomori, who was leading the Taira for Go-Shirakawa. Leading the Minamoto for Sutoku were the clan's head, Tameyoshi, and his son, Tametomo. Tameyoshi's other son, Yoshitomo, was in charge of those Minamoto fighting for Go-Shirakawa. Michinori was Go-Shirakawa's Fujiwara representative and Yorinaga the Fujiwara who fought for Sutoku.

BATTLE TACTICS

So it was that only days after the funeral of ex-emperor Toga, the two rival armies gathered. Go-Shirakawa was based at the imperial palace and Sutoku at Toba's old palace. Tametomo, a young but experienced

Minamoto who was said to have no equal with a bow, suggested that Sutoku make a night attack on the imperial palace. If the emperor could be isolated and even captured, the rebellion would be finished swiftly and decisively. But Yorinaga demurred. He thought they should wait for the arrival of the Nara warrior monks and then negotiate for a pitched battle with Go-Shirakawa's army. Unfortunately, the Nara monks failed to show up, and Yorinaga's dream of a gentlemanly battle fought according to honourable samurai customs was to prove an illusion.

A similar strategy was being shaped at the imperial palace. Fujiwara Michinori agreed with Yoshitomo that they should make a clandestine night attack on Sutoku's headquarters. So it was that early in the morning of 11 July 1156, Go-Shirakawa's force of two Minamoto and one Taira group attacked Toba's palace at three of its four gates. The Minamoto charged with defending the west gate was Tametomo, who, according to legend, headed off the invading force by firing an arrow clean through one attacker and into the man behind him. Kiyomori, who was leading the attack, decided to retreat and regroup, but his young son, Shigemori, had different ideas. In the great samurai tradition, Shigemori called Tametomo out, first by reciting his own lineage and rank and then demanding Tametomo show himself. It was a foolish mistake – Shigemori had never before seen combat, while Tametomo was a hardened Minamoto warrior who had slain many enemies in Emishi country. But before Tametomo could respond, the Go-Shirakawa attack on the gate was redoubled by Tametomo's brother, Yoshitomo.

Yoshitomo called out that he was there under the orders of Emperor Go-Shirakawa to repulse and remove the rebellious gathering before him. Tametomo responded by firing a whistling arrow, which hit Yoshitomo's helmet, taking a piece as it glanced past. After another unsuccessful effort to storm the gate, Yoshitomo decided to burn his brother and father out, and issued the command to set the compound alight. As the old imperial palace blazed, escaping rebel samurai were shot down like rats fleeing a sinking ship. The captured rebel leaders included Sutuko, Tadamasa and the Minamotos – Tameyoshi and Tametomo. The Hōgen Rebellion was over, but it was unclear what punishments would follow.

The samurai of the court, the Fujiwaras, got off lightly. Yorinaga had been killed during the fighting and the other rebel Fujiwara members were sent into exile, as was ex-emperor Sutuko. For Kyoto-loving courtiers, being banished from the city was considered a suitable punishment, but rebel samurai from the provinces would not escape so lightly. Taira Kiyomori was a cold and cruel man, and did not flinch at executing his uncle, Tadamasa. Minamoto Yoshitomo, however, was reluctant to impose the same sentence on his own family. In the end, faced with the dishonourable alternative of allowing a Taira to carry out the order, Yoshitomo instructed a Minamoto samurai to behead his father. Tametomo escaped death by decapitation and was sent into exile, finishing his days by committing the first recorded act of *seppuku*.

In 1158, Emperor Go-Shirakawa decided he would follow his father's lead and abdicate so his teenage son, Nijō, could take the throne and he could rule as cloistered emperor. To outward appearances the whole matter seemed to be resolved, but in actual fact the Hōgen Rebellion was only a prelude to a much bigger conflict that followed.

THE HEIJI REBELLION

While the Hōgen Rebellion had seen various members of different samurai clans fight according to the two imperial factions, the Heiji Rebellion would simply pit clan against clan. For many centuries, there had been a rivalry between the Taira and Minamoto, and it was perhaps surprising that the two had never before come to blows. But while the Heiji Rebellion would set the scene for this, it was only an interlude; a bloody build-up to the bitter Genpei War that was to follow.

The players remaining at the imperial court following the Hōgen Rebellion were Minamoto Yoshitomo, Fujiwara Michinori, Taira Kiyomori and his son, Shigemori. The differences between these men could not have been more pronounced. Michinori was one of Emperor Nijō's chief advisers and a key member of the imperial court. Kiyomori, too, had done his best to ingratiate himself and his family at the court, with the aim of giving the Taira the kind of long-lasting legacy the Fujiwara had enjoyed. Yoshitomo, by comparison, played the courtier, but under the surface he sought revenge for the executions of his father and brother. Besides, no right-thinking Minamoto thought his clan should play second fiddle to the Taira at court. Yoshitomo found an ally in a certain Fujiwara Nobuyori, an ambitious noble who had aspirations to become regent and who hated Kiyomori with a passion. So a plan for another rebellion was hatched between Nobuyori and Yoshitomo.

The plotters waited until Kiyomori and Shigemori had left Kyoto on a pilgrimage, and then set their plan into action on the night of 19 January 1160. Nobuyori, Yoshitomo and a band of elite Minamoto samurai broke into Go-Shirakawa's palace, kidnapped the ex-emperor and set the compound alight. On the other side of Kyoto, a second group of Minamoto set fire to Fujiwara Michinori's house and slaughtered any who tried to flee. As a final act, the rebels stormed Nijō's palace and put the young emperor under house arrest. Nobuyori and Yoshitomo's idea was to coerce Nijō into declaring Kiyomori a rebel and, therefore, escape persecution under the same label. So far the seizure of power had gone according to plan, and now all that remained was to await retaliation by Kiyomori.

A Taira messenger soon reached Kiyomori on the road. The rebels thought Kiyomori would probably head straight for the Kanto plain to raise a formidable Taira force to attack the capital, but instead he travelled straight to Kyoto and arrived unhindered at his own mansion, Rokuhara. He then wrote a courteous note to the rebels at the imperial palace, explaining that he accepted the coup and was at their disposal. Incredibly, Nobuyori and Yoshitomo appeared to take Kiyomori's sentiments as genuine and allowed a number of days to pass without acting against him. This was a fatal error. Since taking over the palace, Nobuyori had developed delusions of grandeur and had also drunk great quantities of the emperor's wine. This had given the 13-year-old Nijō ample time to dress himself as a concubine and escape, along with some real palace women, in an imperial carriage. Spurred on by his son's departure, Go-Shirakawa orchestrated his own escape, simply by dressing as a servant and riding out of the palace.

The news of the royal break-out only reached Yoshitomo's ears because of a rumour that the emperor was safe under Kiyomori's protection at Rokuhara. Yoshitomo was horrified to find not just one but both of his royal prisoners had indeed escaped. Nobuyori was then discovered only a few doors away, rolling drunk among a host of court concubines. Several hundred Taira samurai attacked Nijō's palace and a battle between the Minamoto and Taira ensued, which ended in the pursuit of the Taira all the way back to Rokuhara. It is unclear if this was a ruse by the Taira to lure the Minamoto from the palace, or a result of a direct order from Yoshitomo, but the outcome was the same. The Taira completely outwitted the Minamoto by attacking and then retreating to regroup behind the high Rokuhara walls. Exhausted by this defence and heavily outnumbered, the Minamoto had no option but to flee the city. Yoshitomo and three of his sons rode to the mountains, but were separated by a blizzard. The rebel leader was then betrayed and murdered by one of his retainers while bathing in a mountain hot spring.

Kiyomori's reprisals against the rebels were fast and brutal. Nobuyori and Yoshitomo's son, Yoshihira, were beheaded, as were a number of other Minamoto samurai. Kiyomori agreed to spare Yoshitomo's three other sons, Yoshitsune, Yoritomo and Noriyori, if their mother agreed to become his concubine. While Kiyomori had come out on top following the Hōgen Rebellion, he now looked untouchable. Ironically, the Minamoto had done him an enormous favour by warring with him: Kiyomori had planned to play the long game at court by imitating the Fujiwara strategy of intermarriage to entrench himself and build Taira control; however, instead of waiting years and generations to achieve this goal to outstrip his imperial rivals, Kiyomori had gone straight to the top. He had saved Kyoto from the rebels and, as far as he was concerned, all but rescued Nijō and Go-Shirakawa by himself. The only Minamoto left at court was the aged Yorimasa, who had played no part in the Heiji Rebellion and certainly posed no obvious threat to him.

There was little doubt that Go-Shirakawa was under Kiyomori's control. In 1180 Kiyomori put his 1-year-old grandson on the throne and crowned him Emperor Antoku. Kiyomori set about ruling Japan as regent. Taira domination of power in the capital and the empire was now complete.

4

The Genpei War

THE *GENJI* AND *HEIKE*

While both the Hōgen and Heiji rebellions pitted Taira against Minamoto, their battles were only curtain-raisers for the main event – the Genpei War of 1180–85. This is one of the most famous samurai conflicts in Japanese history and is described in enticing narrative detail in the epic *Heike Monogatari*. The *Heike Monogatari* has been compared to the *Iliad*, recording the heroic exploits of the samurai in vivid poetic detail. On one side are the Taira (*Heike*) with their red flags, and on the other are the Minamoto (*Genji*) with white (these colours would later combine to form the familiar Japanese flag of today). In truth, however, any of the poetic flourishes found in the *Heike Monogatari* cannot disguise the brutal realities of the Genpei War, which would leave one clan officially in charge of the country and the other all but destroyed.

The war began where the Heiji Rebellion left off, at the imperial court where the power-hungry regent, Taira Kiyomori, was ruling through the infant emperor, Antoku. While the appointment had given Kiyomori complete control over the imperial reins, it had left the regent with at least two enemies. One of these was Prince Mochihito, son of the ex-emperor, Go-Shirakawa, who had incorrectly assumed he would inherit the throne. The other was a samurai who Kiyomori felt sure would never be a threat to his rule – the last Minamoto at the Kyoto court, 74-year-old Yorimasa. Yorimasa had stood idle during Kiyomori's purge of the Minamoto clan, and although still a member of the royal court, he had become a laughing stock among his peers. So when the aged samurai sensed that Mochihito had a grudge against Kiyomori, he was quick to sow some revolutionary seeds. The rebel pair waited until Kiyomori and his grandson emperor had left Kyoto on a pilgrimage before Mochihito issued the following proclamation:

The pronouncement of His Excellency the prince declares that Kiyomori, Munemori, and others, using the prestige of their office and their influence, have incited rebellion and have overthrown the nation. They have caused the officials and the people to suffer, seizing and plundering the five inner provinces and the seven circuits. They have confined the ex-sovereign, exiled public officials, and inflicted death and banishment, drowning and imprisonment. They have robbed property and seized lands, usurped and bestowed offices. They have rewarded the unworthy and incriminated the innocent. They have apprehended and confined the prelates of the various temples and imprisoned student monks. They have requisitioned the silks and rice of Mount Hiei to be stored as provisions for a rebellion. They have despoiled the graves of princes and cut off the head of one, defied the emperor and destroyed Buddhist Law in a manner unprecedented in history. Now the country is saddened and the ministers and people alike grieve. In consequence thereof, I, the second son of the ex-sovereign, in search of the ancient principles of Emperor Temmu, and following in the footsteps of Prince Shotoku, proclaim war against those who would usurp the throne and who would destroy Buddhist Law. We rely not on man's efforts alone but on the assistance of providence as well. If the temporal rulers, the Thee Treasures, and the native gods assist us in our efforts, all the people everywhere must likewise wish to assist us immediately.

This being so, let those of the Minamoto, the Fujiwara, and the brave now living in the provinces of the three circuits add their efforts to the cause. If there be those who are not of like mind, they shall be regarded as partisans of Kiyomori and they shall suffer pain of death, exile or imprisonment. If there be those who perform meritoriously, dispatch missions to me and inform me of their names and deeds, and I shall, without fail, following my enthronement, bestow rewards upon them according to their wishes. Proclaim this message in all the provinces and carry out the terms of this pronouncement.[1]

Although it only took two weeks for news of Prince Mochihito's proclamation to reach the travelling Kiyomori, he was not able to see a copy of the text until some days later. As a consequence, he assumed Go-Shirakawa was behind the rebellion and ordered him, as well as Mochihito, to be put under house arrest. But Mochihito, along with Yorimasa and a handful of warrior monks, had fled the capital for Mount Hiei and the Mii-dera temple. Yorimasa set fire to his Kyoto home in a typical samurai act of fatal symbolism – if the rebellion failed, there was no going back.

THE BATTLE OF UJI

It did not take long for Mochihito's proclamation to reach the Minamoto clan in the east. Meanwhile, Yorimasa and Mochihito had arrived at the temple of Mii-dera and bolted the doors in anticipation of Kiyomori's attack. Urgent requests for support were sent from Mii-dera to the neighbouring temple of Enryaku-ji and the *sōhei* of Kōfuku-ji at Nara. In any case, even if these notoriously unreliable priests were to become involved, Mii-dera would not be strong enough to withstand an assault from the mustered Taira, whose samurai army already numbered tens of thousands.

Once again the rebels fled, this time accompanied by around 300 supporters, including Yorimasa's samurai and the Mii-dera *sōhei*. The plan was to retreat to the more fortified temple of Nara, as the defences were better equipped to cope with Kiyomori's army and behind the walls were large numbers of *sōhei*. However, Prince Mochihito was more accustomed to the soft life of the courtier than the frantic scramble of the fugitive. So, on 20 June 1180 the company was forced to rest at the Byodo-in Temple, situated on the banks of the Uji River, which flows south from Lake Biwa. The rebels paused by the temple and ripped planks off the Uji Bridge to stop the advancing Taira force from crossing. However, it was not long before these pursuers caught up to the rebels – perhaps rather too enthusiastically – as the *Heike Monogatari* describes:

> Perceiving that the enemy were at Byodo-in, they raised their warcry three times, when they were answered by that of the Prince's men. The vanguard, seeing the danger, raised a cry of alarm: 'Take care! They have torn up the bridge!' But the rearguard paid no heed and pushed them on with cries of 'Advance! Advance!' so that some two hundred horsemen of the leading company fell through into the river and perished in the stream.[2]

This early action suggests the flow of the river was strong enough to prevent the Taira simply wading across it, and for a time both sides held their ground and fired arrows at each other. The Minamoto were desperately outnumbered and must have hoped the *sōhei* of Nara would make an appearance before the Taira overwhelmed them. Conservative estimates put the size of Kiyomori's force at ten-to-one against that of the rebels, although the *Heike Monogatari* reports there were as many as 28,000 Taira samurai present. But while no Nara *sōhei* had yet emerged to save the day, those Mii-dera *sōhei* on Mochihito's side of the bridge were about to prove their quality.

The warrior monks Gochiin no Tajima and Tsutsui no Jōmyō Meishū had been firing arrows at the enemy so powerfully that 'their shafts pierced them through both shield and armour' when Tajima decided to engage the enemy hand-to-hand, broken bridge or not:

Gochiin no Tajima, throwing away the sheath of his long halberd, strode forth alone on to the bridge, whereupon the Heike straightaway shot at him fast and furious. Tajima, not at all perturbed, ducking to avoid the higher ones and leaping up over those that flew low, cut through those that flew straight with his whirring halberd, so that even the enemy looked on in admiration. Thus it was that he was dubbed 'Tajima the arrow cutter'.[3]

Spurred on by his brother-monk's heroics, Tsutsui no Jōmyō Meishū also sprang onto the bridge, where he proclaimed his rank, title and talents, and shouted that he was 'worth more than a thousand men'. After shooting twelve men dead and wounding a further eleven with his arrows, Jomyo kicked off his shoes and began to navigate his way over the supporting beams of the broken bridge: 'All were afraid to cross over, but he walked as one who walks along the street.'[4] Jomyo then slayed five of the enemy before his *naginata* snapped in two. He then killed eight more with his sword, which also broke in half on his ninth opponent.

Although Jomyo continued the fight with a dagger, his position on the bridge was impeding another warrior monk, Ichirai Hoshi. Hoshi put a hand on Jomyo's helmet and shouted, 'Pardon me Jomyo, this is no good,' and sprang over his shoulder to the front where he fought until he fell. Jomyo himself retreated to the Byodo-in, where he sat down and counted the number of dents the enemy arrows had made in his armour – sixty-three in total, only five of which had passed through. Jomyo's position on the bridge was then taken up by more of the Mii-dera *sōhei*, some of whom, the *Heike Monogatari* reported, returned with the heads of those Taira they had slain. Other *sōhei* who found themselves wounded cut open their stomachs and jumped into the river.

By sundown the broken bridge was strewn with the dead bodies of Taira samurai, and the clan leaders stood nearby and debated how best to ford the river. Some of the older generals suggested the recent rain had made the river impassable and, instead, the troops should cross by the nearest alternative bridge. But the commanders' idea irked Ashikaga no Matataro Tadatsuna, an 18-year-old samurai, who reminded his superiors that taking a detour could allow Yorimasa and Mochihito to escape and give away the Taira's advantage. The battle would still have to be fought another day, only this time the Taira might be facing the combined force of Nara *sōhei* and other Minamoto reinforcements. There was also the question of honour, Ashikaga argued: 'If we do not ford the river here it will be a disgrace to our reputation as samurai; to be drowned is but to die; Forward then!' With these words, Ashikaga led 300 samurai horsemen into the river, barking out orders as they crossed:

> Join hands and go across in line; if your horse's head gets down, pull it up, but don't pull it too far or you will fall off backwards. Sit tight in the saddle and keep your feet firm in the stirrups; where the water is slow and deep get up over the horse's tail; don't shoot while in the water; if the enemy shoots don't draw bow in return; keep your head down and your neck-piece well sloped upwards, but not too far or you will be shot in the crown of the helmet; be light on the horse and firm against the stream; don't go straight across or you will be washed away. [5]

Ashikaga's moment of daring had devastating consequences for the rebels, as the young samurai led his men safely across the Uji and issued the normal battle proclamations to the enemy beyond. Seeing that Ashikaga was now riding up to the Byodo-in Temple and attacking it, the order was given for another Taira contingent to cross the Uji. But these horsemen were not to be so lucky, as the force of the water washed several hundred of them downstream and out of sight.

Meanwhile, a fight to the last man was taking place at the Byodo-in, where the Taira were eagerly taking the heads of those who had fallen. Yorimasa himself was fatally wounded by a volley of arrows and committed *seppuku*. After cutting himself in the usual way he was decapitated by a Minamoto retainer, who threw his weighted head into the Uji River so no Taira could retrieve it. Mochihito tried to escape to Nara on horseback, but was pursued by several hundred Taira samurai; they quickly caught up with the prince, shot him down with arrows and collected his head. The Taira rode back to Kyoto holding hundreds of enemy heads as trophies.

The Minamoto had been too far away to make any sort of late saving appearance, but the Nara *sōhei* were actually coming to the rescue as 'about seven thousand soldier priests of Nara in full armour had gone forth to meet the Prince'.[6] Upon hearing about the day's outcome, however, the *sōhei* turned back to their temples. The first Battle of Uji was over.

PUNISHMENT OF THE PRIESTS

Before Prince Mochihito's rebellion had reached the first hurdle, it had failed. The Minamoto had insufficient time to assemble an army to help and the warrior monks had been too late. As a consequence, it was towards the temples that Kiyomori turned for revenge and reprisals. On 19 December 1180, Taira Tomomori marched 10,000 samurai to the gates of Mii-dera to punish the priests. Around 1,000 Mii-dera monks had prepared a barricade of fallen trees and wooden shields, which they crouched behind with their bows. The battle lasted for the entire day, until at dusk Tomomori's samurai broke through the *sōhei* lines, killed 300 and entered the Mii-dera monastery. Mii-dera was then set alight and 2,000 of its buildings burned to the ground; two statues of Buddha and several thousand volumes of the Holy Sutras were also lost in the blaze.

There was anguish and outrage from the priests of Nara when they heard of Kiyomori's sacrilege. Expecting a backlash from Nara, Kiyomori sent an envoy for talks with the priests, who travelled to Nara inside one of the court's finest carriages. This failed to impress the priests of Kōfuku-ji, who pulled the envoy from the carriage, beat him, shaved his head and sent him back to the capital. The angry monks then carved a wooden head called Kiyomori and kicked it around the temple grounds. Despite this, Kiyomori must have still hoped to engage the priests in peace talks, as he sent 500 Taira samurai to Kōfuku-ji with explicit instructions to engage only in discussion and not violence. The Nara priests were either unaware of this order or indifferent to it: they seized sixty of the Taira samurai, decapitated them and stuck their heads on display outside the temple gates. Kiyomori reacted to this incident with predictable fury:

'Now I will certainly attack the South Capital,' the regent said, and sent an army of 40,000 mounted samurai to deal with Nara once and for all.

All the 7,000 monks of Kōfuku-ji could do was fortify their temple by digging ditches, building earthworks and erecting palisades, and then stand in wait. When the army arrived on 28 December 1180, the Taira split their force in two and attacked Kōfuku-ji in waves until they broke through the line of defending monks. Then, as with Mii-dera, the Taira set Kōfuku-ji alight. It was a windy day and, as the *Heike Monogatari* recounts, the buildings went up fast:

> The wind was blowing strongly, so that although only one place was set on fire, owing to the wind veering about in all directions, the flames spread hither and thither and most of the temple buildings were soon in a blaze. By this time all the warrior monks who scorned to surrender for fear of dishonour had fallen fighting ... Those who were too old to flee, and the unattached laymen, children and girls, thinking to save themselves, went up into the upper story of the Daibutsuden or fled into the interior of Yamashinadera in their panic. About a thousand of them crowded into the Daibutsuden and pulled up the ladders behind them so that the enemy could not follow, but the flames reached them first, and such a great crying arose as could not be surpassed even by the sinners amid the flames of Tapana, Pratapana and Avitchi, the fiercest of the Eight Hot Hells.[7]

The next temple to be razed was Tōdai-ji, which still housed the statue of Buddha commissioned by Emperor Shotoku 400 years earlier. By the end the statue was little more than a shapeless lump of metal standing among the smouldering ruins of the monastery. Over 3,500 had perished, including 1,000 *sōhei*, whose heads now adorned what was left of the temple gates.

Kiyomori reportedly rejoiced openly at the news of the carnage, while the rest of the court fell into a sorrowful silence. The regent then began to have vivid nightmares and visions which seemed to have been dispatched from hell itself. Kiyomori had moved the emperor to a new

temporary capital at Fukuhara as a precaution against what he assumed
was an imminent Minamoto invasion, and it was here, among the walls
of his newly built palace, that he experienced aural hallucinations – the
sounds of timbers crashing around him and the laughter of thousands of
people. Then Kiyomori had a vision in the palace grounds:

> One morning when Kiyomori went out of his chamber and passed
> through the wicket gate to view the garden, at once the garden was filled
> with a heap of skulls of dead men without number that rolled and writhed
> one over another, up and down and in and out, rattling and clattering
> as they moved. The Nyudo [Kiyomori] called to his attendants, but it
> chanced that there was no one to answer. Then all the skulls came together
> and united into one huge skull like a mountain in size, that seemed to fill
> the whole garden, perhaps a hundred and forty or fifty feet high, and in
> this great skull appeared millions of great eyes like the eyes of a man, that
> glared at the Nyudo with an unwinking stare.[8]

Kiyomori stationed a guard of fifty men by day and a hundred at night to
fire whistling arrows to scare off any supernatural spirits or evil demons.
While these apparitions may have been only a result of Kiyomori
struggling with his conscience, it was hard to escape the ill omens for the
Taira clan.

MINAMOTO YORITOMO

By the time the Minamoto reacted to Mochihito's proclamation, the
prince and Yorimasa were both dead, and news of their demise at the
Battle of Uji was relayed with varying degrees of accuracy. Some of these
reports even told of a Yorimasa victory and Prince Mochihito's imminent
arrival in the east. But even so, it still appeared that there was an uprising
against Kiyomori and that the Minamoto needed to prepare an army.

The samurai chosen to lead the Minamoto was none other than
Yoritomo, Yoshitomo's eldest son, who had been spared by Kiyomori

after the Heiji Rebellion. Kiyomori had exiled the young Yoritomo in 1160 to the Taira-occupied Izu Peninsula. Here, he was brought up under the guardianship of Fujiwara and Hōjō samurai, who were allies of the Taira court. Despite this, Yoritomo's life was far from oppressive – the young man was encouraged to learn the arts and the theory of war, and even allowed to marry the Hōjō samurai's daughter. Yoritomo became a bright, educated and charismatic young man, who was a natural choice to lead an army against the tyrant who had murdered his father. So when a copy of Mochihito's proclamation found its way to Izu, Yoritomo felt his time had come.

In September 1180, the young Minamoto fled the peninsula with a handful of supporters, but hot on his tail was samurai Ōba Kagechika, whose small force of tough Taira veterans caught up with Yoritomo at the Ishibashiyama Valley. Here, under the cover of darkness, Kagechika decimated Yoritomo's bodyguard, though he failed to catch the young Minamoto leader. Yoritomo had managed to escape on horseback, and would not stop riding until he had mustered a large army and reached his father's old base at Kamakura. Yoritomo's samurai army would include members of the Hōjō, among other Minamoto allies, and news of its formation eventually reached a furious Kiyomori. The regent immediately commanded a contingent of Taira samurai, led by his grandson, Koremori, to march out and meet Yoritomo's army. So it was set that the two great Japanese clans would meet each other on the banks of the Fuji River for the first great pitched battle of the Genpei War.

The battle, however, was never to take place. The Minamoto army, which according to the *Heike Monogatari* was over 200,000 strong, certainly outnumbered that of the Taira. The Taira knew this only too well, marvelling at the size of the Minamoto camp the night before the supposed battle and describing it as 'without number'. This created consternation among the Taira warriors, and they were certainly jumpy when, later that night, a flock of water fowl were disturbed by a small advance party of Minamoto warriors. Fearing an imminent massacre was upon them, the Taira panicked:

So, panic-stricken, they abandoned their positions and fled precipitately without even taking their belongings with them, for so great was their haste that some snatched up their bows without any arrows, or arrows without any bow, springing on to each other's horses, and even mounting tethered animals and whipping them up so that they galloped round and round the post to which they were tied. There were some too who had procured some singing girls and courtesans, and were banqueting and making merry with them when the alarm took place, and these women were hustled and thrown down and trampled on in the confusion, so that they were injured in the head or body and added their cries to the uproar.[9]

The Taira withdrawal from the site of battle caused a major loss of face for the samurai at court. Kiyomori himself was so mortified by the news that he fell into what the *Heike Monogatari* describes as 'a most extraordinary sickness':

On the twenty-eighth day it was reported that his condition was grave, and all Rokuhara and the Capital was in an uproar, every one running about and whispering together. From the day that the Nyudo was taken ill, he could not drink even hot water, and the heat of his body was like a burning fire, so that if any one came within eight or ten yards of him the heat was unbearable. All he could do was to mutter 'Ata! Ata' ['Hot! Hot!']: it was a most extraordinary sickness. To relieve him somewhat they brought water from the well of Senshuin of Hieizan and filled a stone tank with it, into which they lowered him, but the water began to bubble and boil and immediately became like a hot bath. When water was poured on him from a pipe, it flew off again hissing in clouds of steam and spray as though it had struck red hot iron or stone, and the water that did strike him burst into flames so that the whole chamber was filled with whirling fires and thick black smoke.[10]

It must have been obvious to Kiyomori that he had missed his opportunity to stop the Minamoto uprising; but despite the retreat, it was clear that Kiyomori's fledgling Taira force, commanded by his inexperienced courtier grandson, would have been no match for the hardened Minamoto. Nevertheless, this had not moved Kiyomori to make any attempt to reconcile feelings between the rival Taira and Minamoto clans. After all, the main protagonists in the rebellion – Prince Mochihito and Minamoto Yorimasa – were now both dead. There was no reason the two clans could not have continued as before, with the Taira ruling the capital and the Minamoto the dominant clan of Kanto. Instead, Kiyomori had gone out of his way to provoke bad feelings between the clans and now civil war was upon him. As news reached Kiyomori's death-bed that the Minamoto army was marching on the capital, the Taira regent, burning with fever and bitterness, finally died. His departing words were not of guilt or remorse, but a final order to the Taira clan:

> The only thing I have to regret is that I cannot see the head of Hyoye-no-suke Yoritomo. When I am dead do not perform any Buddhist services or make offerings for me, or build temples or pagodas; only make haste and slay Yoritomo and cut off his head and lay it before my tomb. That will be the best offering you can make me either in this world or the next.[11]

MINAMOTO YOSHINAKA

If the Taira thought they could end the Genpei War by removing the Minamoto leader, Yoritomo, they were wrong. For although Yoritomo appeared to be the commander of the Minamoto at his Kamakura headquarters, there were other family members with armies and ideas of their own. One of these was Yoritomo's brother, Yukiie, and the other was his cousin, Yoshinaka.

Yoshinaka is one the heroes of samurai legend whose adventures began when he was an infant. Born a Minamoto, Yoshinaka lost his father in 1155 during a samurai battle and was then brought up by adoptive parents in the province of Kiso, Shinano. A true child of the countryside, Yoshinaka is described as being physically strong, bold and unimpressed by the proud behaviour displayed by those in the capital. Yoshinaka was also often regarded as Yoritomo's polar opposite – coarse, uneducated and uninterested in courtly manners or etiquette. There was no love lost between the cousins.

The two did share similar ambitions, though: like Yoritomo, Yoshinaka took Prince Mochihito's proclamation as a call to arms and quickly raised a Minamoto army to fight the Taira. However, he was unwilling to serve under Yoritomo's generalship and, instead, maintained his own force at Shinano, about 50 miles from the capital. Yoshinaka was so successful in conquering the Taira counties surrounding Shinano that Yoritomo began to fear he would lead an uprising against him. Yoshinaka had refused to recognise his cousin as overall leader of the Minamoto and, in 1183, Yoritomo sent his army for talks. An inter-clan war was only just avoided after lengthy negotiations, which concluded with Yoshinaka sending his son to Kamakura as a hostage.

The treaty was fortunate as, only weeks later, a massive Taira force marched out from Kyoto on Yoshinaka's vastly inferior army. This began a series of attacks and retreats by the Minamoto in a strategic ploy to stretch the Taira supply line and undermine their enthusiasm. While the Taira viewed the early months of 1183 as a culmination of victories against a fleeing enemy, their fortunes would turn in June at a mountain gorge in Kurikara. The subsequent battle represents the two sides of samurai warfare: on one side are honourable ideals and principles; on the other, ruthlessness, cunning and deception. The battle would end in absolute victory for Yoshinaka, who would then march on Kyoto itself (see page 112).

Those in the capital reacted with shock and panic to news of the Taira retreat. Emperor Antoku was hurried away clutching the three sacred imperial treasures of power that every legitimate emperor was supposed to have in his possession – the sword, mirror and jewel. Many Kyoto homes, such as Kiyomori's mansion, Rokuhara, were torched as the Taira nobles fled, though some of those wishing to meet the attackers remained. Ex-emperor Go-Shirakawa simply sent word from his residence welcoming the Minamoto. After the battle was won in the month of August 1183, the triumphant Yoshinaka marched through the streets of Kyoto.

The moment was a shock for both sides. Japan had had its share of natural disasters, and famine and pestilence had been raging for months. So, instead of cheering crowds and banquets, Yoshinaka and his men found a city exhausted by starvation. As it happened, the disappointment was not one-sided as, while Kyoto's suffering inhabitants may have been expecting a regiment of conquering heroes, what they actually saw was a ramshackle parade of bedraggled and war-weary soldiers. There were to be further surprises when Yoshinaka, well known as the cousin of the well-educated and cultured Yoritomo, turned out to be a boorish clod. The *Heike Monogatari* describes him thus:

> He was of fair complexion and handsome appearance, it is true, but his manners and way of speaking were rough and unpolished in the extreme. For this indeed there was good reason; for how could anyone be other who had been brought up from the age of two until over thirty in the wild mountain country of Kiso?[12]

Things only got worse for Yoshinaka: first, he mercilessly taunted a court official for having a name like a cat's; and then headed off to the royal palace dressed in clothes that made him look 'ridiculous in the extreme'.[13] He then needed to be shown how to ride in an ox-car and reprimanded a servant who tried to explain the correct procedure for alighting from a carriage: 'It is my car,' remonstrated Yoshinaka, 'so I shall do as I please.'

Yoshinaka planned to behave exactly as he liked and this extended far beyond breaches of etiquette. Instead, Yoshinaka and his men began to roam around the city, pillaging and attacking those who resisted. Relations between Yoshinaka and Go-Shirakawa soon became strained to breaking point. Go-Shirakawa was horrified by Yoshinaka and wrote to Yoritomo imploring him to control his cousin. Yoshinaka was far beyond being told what to do by his distant cousin and, instead, attempted to seize the capital for himself. He put Go-Shirakawa under house arrest, decapitated over a hundred Taira courtiers and placed their heads on display. He even sought out an alliance with the Taira enemy to fight Yoritomo, leaving him with no option but to send a large force to deal with Yoshinaka. This army would be commanded by Yoritomo's brother, Minamoto Yoshitsune, one of the most famous heroes of samurai legend (see page 129).

On hearing of Yoshitsune's approach, Yoshinaka ordered his army to the Uji River, where he hoped to head off his rivals. Following the example set by Minamoto Yorimasa in 1180, Yoshinaka's men tore up the planks of the bridge and then added some sharp stakes to the riverbed to prevent horsemen from crossing. Yet, even the swollen waters of the Uji could not stop Yoshitsune's men from riding across it, and the battle was quickly won. Yoshinaka himself had stayed in Kyoto during the proceedings, but soon received word that the victorious Yoshitsune was marching towards him. The *Heike Monogatari* describes this advance, with the valiant Yoshitsune galloping into the palace courtyard to offer his protection to the beaming Go-Shirakawa.

As this was all taking place, Yoshinaka rode out from the capital with only seven retainers, one of them a woman – Tomoe Gozen. Gozen's inclusion is notable, not just because she is a woman samurai, but also because of her unflinching display of loyalty to the doomed Yoshinaka (see page 133).

Yoshinaka's last stand sees him ready to ride out for death and glory against 6,000 enemy samurai as one of his retainers, Imai Kanehira, pleads with him to take the honourable path of *seppuku*: 'My lord is weary and his charger also, and if, as may be, he meet his death at the hands of some low retainer, how disgraceful that it should be.' The *Heike Monogatari* describes Yoshinaka's final moments:

He had not gone far before his horse plunged heavily into the muddy ooze beneath. Right up to the neck it floundered, and though Kiso [Yoshinaka] plied whip and spur with might and main, it was all to no purpose, for he could not stir it. Even in this plight he still thought of his retainer, and was turning to see how it fared with Imai, when Miura-no-Ishida Jiro Tamehisa of Sagami rode up and shot an arrow that struck him in the face under his helmet. Then as the stricken warrior fell forward in his saddle that his crest bowed over his horse's head, two of Ishida's retainers fell upon him and struck off his head.[14]

Kanehira was still fighting when he heard his master had been slain, crying out his last words to his foes: '"Alas, for whom now have I to fight? See, you fellows of the East Country, I will show you how the mightiest champion in Nippon can end his life!" And he thrust the point of his sword in his mouth and flung himself headlong from his horse, so that he was pierced through and died.' And as Yoshinaka's chapter ended, so began the final chapter of the Genpei War.

TAIRA IN RETREAT

After Yoshitsune returned to Kyoto with Yoshinaka's head, he was ordered by Yoritomo to ride out and destroy the Taira. The Taira had abandoned their headquarters at Fukuhara for their fortress at Ichinotani, which was protected by the sea on one side and cliffs and palisades on the other. Of all the samurai clans, the Taira were the masters of the sea, and their navy lay in the waters beside Ichinotani to enable a quick retreat if needed.

On approaching Ichinotani, Yoshitsune split his troops into two groups: 7,000 would attack the sea-facing side; and he would personally lead a smaller contingent to the cliffs on the eastern side. This caused immediate consternation among those heading east, as one samurai commented in the *Heike Monogatari*: 'Everyone knows the dangers of that place; if we must die, it were better to die facing the foe than to fall over a cliff and be killed. Does anyone know the way among these mountains?'

Luckily for Yoshitsune, there happened to be an old hunter on the mountain above the eastern face who knew the area well. The hunter explained that the way from their position on the mountain into the Taira fort at the bottom was blocked by a steep impasse. Moreover, the last 100m of this impasse was a sheer drop down a cliff face. On closer interrogation, however, the hunter admitted that stags were known to find their way down: 'Forsooth!' exclaimed Yoshitsune, 'then a horse can do it, for where a stag may pass, there a horse can go also.' So it was that Yoshitsune and his 3,000 men descended into the unprotected rear of Ichinotani and sowed panic among those inside the fortress.

Somehow a defensive line was formed against the Minamoto attackers, who engaged the Taira and began setting fire to the fortress buildings. Seeing the black plumes of smoke rising from Ichinotani, many Taira samurai bolted for their ships. As a result, the ships quickly became overloaded and pandemonium ensued:

> Moreover those in the ships would only take on board those warriors who were of high rank, and thrust away the common soldiers, slashing at them with their swords and halberds, but even though they saw this, rather than stay and be cut down by the enemy, they clung to the ships and strove to drag themselves on board, so that their hands and arms were cut off and they fell back into the sea, which quickly reddened with their blood.[15]

Despite the demise of large numbers of Taira during the Battle of Ichinotani, there had been enough time to bundle Emperor Antoku into a boat and whisk him away to the Taira's next fortress at Yashima. The Taira defeat also provided a respite in the fighting, as Yoshitsune waited for reinforcements from Kamakura. It was actually some months later that Yoshitsune set sail from Honshu to the coast of Shikoku, where Yashima sat high on a rocky ridge of headland.

The Minamoto required a navy if they were to pursue their foe once more. This created a stir among the Minamoto men – the first time there was dissent over Yoshitsune's military decisions. One of Yoshitsune's generals, Kajiwara Kagetoki, suggested to his commander that the boats be equipped with extra oars at the bow and stern to enable an escape if necessary. His advice annoyed Yoshitsune, who barked that armies never set out with the notion of retreating and that his ship would be equipped only with forward-facing oars. The *Heike Monogatari* recounts Kagetoki's reply: 'A good general is one who advances at the proper time, and retreats at the proper time, thus saving his own life and destroying the enemy – that is what is called a good general. But a man of only one idea is called a "wild-boar-warrior" and is not thought much of.' The two nearly came to blows, but Yoshitsune eventually shrugged it off. However, Kagetoki was annoyed enough to send Yorimoto a full account of the 'wild-boar warrior' in command, with consequences far outlasting the Battle of Yashima.

In many ways, the battle itself was a non-event. The Minamoto approached the Taira cautiously from the shore, while the Taira rained down arrows from the decks of their ships. The Taira hung a fan from a pole on one of their boats as an archery challenge – or rather a trap to entice Yoshitsune himself to take the shot, thus making him a target. Yoshitsune's skill as an archer was not revealed until later, when he dropped his bow in the sea and took great pains to retrieve it. His reason, it transpired, was that his bow was not strung by three men 'like that of my uncle Tametomo. They would be quite welcome to it – but I should not like a weak one like mine to fall into the hands of the enemy for them to laugh at it.'

In the *Heike Monogatari*, Yoshitsune's explanation about the bow 'drew expressions of approval from all' rather than laughter at their commander's apparent weakness, a telling point about the absolute necessity for a samurai not to lose face. The Battle of Yashima soon petered out as the Taira once again took to their ships. Their final confrontation with the Minamoto would take place at the last of their fortresses at Dannoura.

THE BATTLE OF DANNOURA

The Taira base of Dannoura stood at the very end of Honshu, with only a small strait separating it from the island of Kyūshū. While the Taira tried to buoy themselves over their chances, it was obvious that Dannoura would be the clan's last stand. The Taira did have the advantage at sea, but they had reached the end of Japanese soil and there was nowhere to escape.

The Minamoto had been joined by many ally ships as its fleet sailed along the Inland Sea towards Dannoura. Realising the Minamoto navy now far outnumbered its own, the Taira commander, Tomomori, prepared for a battle in the strait next to the Dannoura fortress. Tomomori's plan was to put Emperor Antoku onboard a plain ship and use the imperial flagship as a decoy; the flagship would then be used to draw the

Minamoto fleet into an exposed position. The Taira samurai were told to target Yoshitsune himself, who was easy to recognise as a 'little fellow with a fair complexion and his front teeth stick out a bit'.

There was one last precaution that Tomomori wanted to take – to chop off their ally Awa no Mimbu Shigeyoshi's head. Tomomori had grave reservations about Shigeyoshi's strength of character, which he brought to the attention of the Taira commander-in-chief, Munemori. Munemori called Shigeyoshi to him: 'How now, Shigeyoshi? Do you intend treachery? said Munemori, 'for your conduct today has a suspicious look. Do tell your men of Shikoku to bear themselves well in the fight, and don't play the dastard.'

Shigeyoshi protested his innocence to Munemori as Tomomori stood to one side 'with his hand gripping his sword hilt hard enough to break it, casting meaningful looks at Munemori to intimate his wish to cut Shigeyoshi down'. But the order for Tomomori to execute Shigeyoshi did not come, and this was to be the Taira's undoing.

So, on 24 April 1185, the Minamoto and Taira ships met for the final battle of the Genpei War. The Taira fleet used the ocean currents to bear down on the Minamoto and the sky was made dark with the clouds of arrows fired from either side. The Taira were trying to pick out Yoshitsune as instructed and leave the Minamoto without their leader, while the Minamoto were trying to destroy the large Chinese galleys which they assumed the Taira commanders would be aboard. Instead, the commanders and their elite samurai had sailed out in the plain fighting boats to rally and board the ships of the Minamoto.

This was the moment, as predicted, that Shigeyoshi defected from the Taira and joined the Minamoto, taking many of his men with him. Shigeyoshi's first move was to give away the Taira battle tactics and Yoshitsune quickly commanded his men to use their arrows on the sailors and rowers, not the Taira samurai themselves. This threw the Taira fleet into confusion – some boats were left floating aimlessly, while others were pulled away from the battle by the currents. From the deck of the ship carrying the emperor, it was clear that all was lost. His mother grabbed the young emperor in her arms and stood by the side of the boat, inspiring one of the most famous lines in samurai history: 'There is a pure land of happiness beneath the waves, another capital where no sorrow is. Thither it is that I am taking Our Lord in the depths of the ocean where we have a capital.' And with this, the two sank beneath the waves.

Antoku's mother would actually be pulled back up, as a Minamoto samurai on a dinghy caught her hair in a rake. The 7-year-old Emperor Antoku, however, was lost forever, along with the sacred imperial sword, although the mirror and jewel were recovered. The emperor's death signalled the end of the battle, and of the Taira: the clan was almost totally destroyed by an act of mass suicide. Before jumping into the waves, many Taira wrapped themselves in chains, anchors or double layers of armour to ensure they would sink:

> And now the whole sea was red with the banners and insignia that they tore off and cut away, so that it looked like the waters of the Tatsuta-gawa when it is flecked with the maple leaves that the wind brings down in autumn, while the white breakers that rolled up on the beach were dyed a scarlet colour. The deserted empty ships rocked mournfully on the waves, driven aimlessly hither and thither by the wind and tide.[16]

For centuries the waters around Dannoura were avoided by sailors and fishermen, who feared the souls of the suicidal samurai would suck them beneath the waves. The faces of the dead are said to be etched onto the shells of the Heike crabs which are still found in the area today.

It would be reasonable to predict an epilogue to the Genpei War in which the victorious Yoshitsune was given a hero's welcome in Kyoto and Kamakura, and awarded a prestigious title and large parcel of land. Instead, Yoritomo, spurred by jealousy and Kagetoki's damning 'wild-boar' report, issued a warrant for his cousin's arrest. Yoshitsune was thereafter forced to live as a wanted fugitive and outlaw, until finally meeting his end in 1189.

Yoritomo was given the post of *shōgun*, or 'Barbarian-subduing commander-in-chief', by the new teenage emperor Go-Toba. This would usher in a new feudal age where Japan was controlled exclusively by the samurai. For the next 750 years, Japan's emperors would only have theoretical authority and, instead, play puppet to the real ruler, the *shōgun*. In the end, Yoritomo, unlike his relatives who won the Genpei War on his behalf, suffered a less than heroic end: he fell off his horse in 1199 and died from his injuries. Popular folklore had it that the ghost of Yoshitsune had spooked Yoritomo's horse, making it rear back and unseat its master.

NOTES

1   *Heike Monogatari*
2   Ibid.
3   Ibid.
4   Ibid.
5   Ibid.
6   Ibid.
7   Ibid.
8   Ibid.
9   Ibid.
10 Ibid.
11 Ibid.
12 Ibid.
11 Ibid.
12 Ibid.
13 Ibid.
14 Ibid.
15 Ibid.
16 Ibid.

5

Medieval Japan

KAMAKURA PERIOD (1185–1333)

The great irony of the Minamoto's bloody rise to power is that it would not last. Yoritomo's unexpected demise in 1199 had left his son, Yoriie, as *shōgun*, but at only 18 he was considered too young to rule. Instead, actual control lay with the regent, or *shikken*, which in this case was Yorimoto's widow, Hōjō Masako. This created a bizarre hierarchy where a *shikken* ruled on behalf of the *shōgun*, who ruled on behalf of the emperor. Despite the Hōjō's control of the regency, however, the title of *shōgun* would stay under the Minamoto name until 1867.

Yoriie fell sick and was assassinated in 1204, and, although Yoriie's son, Kugyo, was next in line, power went to Yoriie's younger brother, Sanetomo. However, Sanetomo was stabbed to death one snowy morning on the steps of Kamakura's Hachiman shrine. Suspicion fell on Kugyo and, guilty or not, he was executed the same day; as the last Minamoto in line, Kugyo's demise also meant the end of Minamoto rule over Japan. The clan which had fought so hard against the Taira for control had itself been destroyed within just thirty years, and, from then on, the Minamoto would hold the shōgunate in name only.

The Hōjō clan would continue to rule as regents for the next century, but there was unrest between the imperial court and the clan, and ex-emperor Go-Toba tried to raise an army against the regent in 1221. The ensuing mini-conflict, known as the Jōkyū War, in some ways resembled the Genpei conflict. Go-Toba issued a proclamation renouncing the Hōjō leader, Yoshitoki, and even fought a third battle at the Uji Bridge against him. It ended quickly, with Yoshitoki's army marching down the streets of Kyoto in victory. The incident is, however, notable as the precursor to the ongoing power struggle between the emperor and the *shōgun*. This would come to a head in the early fourteenth century and see the Hōjō deposed. Of course, emperor and *shōgun* were only nominal titles – the real power belonged to the regent and the cloistered ex-emperor standing in the shadows.

Before this power struggle took place, Japan became embroiled in one of the major events of the thirteenth century – the Mongol Invasion. This catastrophe forced warring Japan to curtail its internal squabbling and unite against the foreign foe.

THE MONGOL INVASION

The first sign of trouble came in 1266 when two emissaries from China brought a letter addressed to the 'King of Japan'. The letter had been written by Kublai Khan, grandson of Genghis, who had recently conquered most of China and Korea. The letter was polite, but clear in its instruction:

> The Great Mongol emperor sends this letter to the King of Japan. The sovereigns of small countries, sharing borders with each other, have for a long time been concerned to communicate with each other and become friendly. Especially since my ancestor governed at heaven's command,

innumerable countries from afar disputed our power and slighted our virtue … Our relation is feudatory like a father and son. We think you already know this … however, Japan has never dispatched ambassadors since my ascending the throne. It is horrifying to think that the Kingdom is yet to know this. Hence we dispatched a mission with our letter particularly expressing our wishes. Enter into friendly relations with each other from now on. We think all countries belong to one family. How are we in the right, unless we comprehend this? Nobody would wish to resort to arms.[1]

Kublai's letter both terrified and insulted the imperial court – it was, after all, addressed to the 'King' and not the 'Emperor' of Japan. The Hōjō in Kamakura, the real seat of power, were less concerned. Samurai had been honing their fighting skills on each other for centuries and they relished the idea of fighting an enemy on behalf of the whole nation.

So the official line to China was 'thank-you, but we're not really interested', while the Hōjō began readying itself for a hostile Chinese response. The *shōgun*'s regent at that time, 18-year-old Hōjō Tokimune, wasted no time in preparing fortifications around Hakata Bay on the island of Kyūshū. This was the most likely landing point for a foreign army and the inhabitants were moved westwards. Meanwhile, Kublai tried further diplomacy by sending several Chinese emissaries between 1268 and 1272. At first his envoys were told Japan was not interested in becoming a vassal state to China; and later their ships were simply not permitted to land. So, in 1274, Kublai's Mongol fleet set sail for Japan.

Kublai sent 700 ships, carrying 15,000 Mongol and Chinese warriors, and 10,000 Korean soldiers. The first island to receive the foreign conquerors was Tsushima, halfway between Korea and Japan. Here, the Chinese army showed it would not adhere to samurai rules of honourable conduct in war. Instead, it marched ashore, massacred any inhabitants it could find and burnt the villages to the ground. The women were raped and then hung from the Chinese masts by wire forced through their hands. This was the human shield that confronted the samurai when the Mongols entered Hakata Harbour a few days later.

While some samurai charged out to meet the landing Chinese boats, it quickly became clear that the samurai mode of one-to-one combat would not prevail against this foreign enemy. The Mongols fired volley after volley of poisoned arrows, and used large catapults to hurl exploding iron bombs. After a bitter day of fighting on Hakata beach, the samurai retreated to nearby fortifications and the Mongols went back to their ships. Although the day had belonged to the Mongols, they feared a night attack on land and felt their ships offered better protection. The decision proved to be their undoing, as the wind picked up and a great storm approached. The fleet pulled out of the harbour and into the open sea, but many ships were smashed on the rocky headland and others were lost in a rising swell. By the time the bewildered samurai emerged from hiding, all that remained of the fleet were stranded ships and wrecks. There was no-one left to fight – Kublai's surviving army had sailed home.

The samurai quickly reinforced their battlements, building a vast 2m-high stone wall around the shoreline. A crack squad kept a coastal watch and they waited for another wave of marauding Mongols. Kublai once again tried the diplomatic route. In 1275 a ship carrying five Chinese emissaries landed and refused to leave until the emperor had listened to their message; they were sent to Kamakura and promptly beheaded. In 1279 a further five envoys sailed into Hakata, where they met the same fate. So in 1281, an enraged Kublai once again sent a fleet of ships to destroy his enemy.

This time the Mongol fleet sailed in two parts: the first, of 900 Korean ships, carried more than 40,000 men; the other, comprising 3,500 ships, carried 100,000 men. The Korean fleet sailed directly to invade Tsushima Island and then Iki Island, before heading to Hakata. Here they made a landing of sorts at the southern end of the newly built wall, but opposition to the invaders was far fiercer than it had been six years earlier and Kublai's men failed to retain a foothold on Kyūshū. The samurai mounted hit-and-run attacks on the Korean ships: a dozen men on a small boat would approach a larger enemy ship by stealth, board it and behead everyone they met. Then before the alarm could be raised, the warriors would retreat to their boat and return to shore with their tally of trophy heads. These skirmishes would often take place at night, but on one occasion a boat sailed in daylight, pretending to surrender. When the Korean ship lowered a gangplank to help the apparently unarmed men, the samurai suddenly produced their weapons and slaughtered all on board.

The main Chinese force arrived some weeks later and avoided Hakata altogether, instead landing some miles to the south. Here, the ships roped together to form a floating headquarters at sea, while raiding parties went ashore in smaller vessels, attacking and burning villages. Then something remarkable happened that neither side could have anticipated, but which the samurai later regarded as an act of providence. They called the storm which wrecked the Mongol fleet *kamikaze*, or 'divine wind'. This terrible monsoon ravaged the coastline for two days, tossing the Mongol ships around like corks and smashing them to pieces. When the winds finally subsided, the samurai reported that the water was so thick with corpses that they could walk across it. The Mongols who survived were quickly rounded up and beheaded.

Although there was further talk about suppressing the 'rebellious Japanese', Kublai Khan failed to do so and died in 1294. The Mongol invasions proved to be the first of only two occasions when the samurai had to fight foreign soldiers; the second would be their invasion of Korea in the late sixteenth century. By 1281 the Mongols had been repelled, and the clans of Japan were free once more to start fighting with one another.

IMPERIAL REVOLUTIONS

The Hōjō emerged from the Mongol conflicts as the saviours of Japan and proved the need for a *bakufu*, or temporary shōgunal government. But in 1281 Hōjō Tokimune, the commander who had led the samurai against the barbarians, died, and the principles that had made the Hōjō a formidable *bakufu* — honour, pride, strength and efficiency — died with him. By 1318, the regent was Hōjō Takatoki, whose main interests were dancing and dog-fighting. Watching the Hōjō command's lapse into luxury and debauchery was the ambitious and opportunistic Emperor Go-Daigo.

Go-Daigo was Takatoki's nemesis – a motivated and ambitious emperor who saw the *bakufu* as an unwelcome imposter with no business interfering in imperial rule. Go-Daigo's main objective was to reverse the role of the emperor from shōgunal puppet to a true and proper sovereign with real power over his empire. As a first step, Go-Daigo abolished the Insei system of cloistered rule: from then on the emperor would be the real ruler, not just a figurehead. Go-Daigo's next step would be to return full authority to the emperor, and Takatoki's failure to resolve a dispute between two members of the Ando clan in 1322 provided the opportunity. The Hōjō samurai sent to settle the matter were killed and beheaded by the Ando, requiring Takatoki to send a second and larger force. For Takatoki this was no great matter, but for Go-Daigo it was proof that the *bakufu* was not doing its job.

In the following years, Go-Daigo cultivated relations with those opposed to the Kamakura *bakufu*, which included the warrior monks of Mount Hiei and Nara. It would take several years for the Hōjō to finally act on intelligence that Go-Daigo was raising an army against them, but by the time the *bakufu* army marched into Kyoto in 1331 to suppress Go-Daigo, the emperor had stolen away to the Tōdai-ji temple at Nara.

The Hōjō army assumed Go-Daigo had sought refuge with his son, the abbot of Enryaku-ji, and attacked the monastery there. The ensuing battle was a decisive victory for the *bakufu*, but the abbot, Prince Morinaga, escaped to the fortress of Akasaka in Kawachi. Akasaka was the stronghold of Kusunoki Masashige, a famous samurai celebrated for his imperial loyalty. Masashige was a rare breed of samurai who actually supported the emperor himself, and not the shōgunate clan that represented him.

By this time, samurai methods of fighting were changing. The Mongol conflict had shown that not all opponents were willing to play by the honourable rules of samurai battle. Kublai's hostile intentions had not been announced through the firing of whistling arrows; nor had Chinese warriors called out their name, rank and position to attract a suitable samurai of similar standing. Instead, the Mongols had been cruel, calculating and cunning, and the samurai had had to respond in kind. Moreover, this new and improvised form of warfare seemed to rub off on the samurai, who adopted the Mongols' tactics when fighting each other.

The Siege of Akasaka in 1331 is a good example of the new style. Akasaka was described as a fortress, but in reality it was little more than a stockade with earthworks, tall palisades and wooden watchtowers. These apparently flimsy battlements enticed the Hōjō into charging the walls, but they were quickly repulsed by a volley of arrows fired not just from Akasaka, but a nearby neighbouring hill. Masashige also used boiling water, and large rolling logs and boulders against the besieging Hōjō. The Hōjō responded by blocking Akasaka's water supply. In a previous conflict the samurai army left starving inside the fortress walls might have responded by committing mass *seppuku*, and this was also in Masashige's mind – but as a ploy to enable his army to escape. Masashige built a funeral pyre with the bodies of his dead and then secretly retreated with his men through a back gate. One lone samurai stayed behind to relay a tearful story to the advancing Hōjō of the tragic group suicide, indicating that what remained of Masashige's army was now a burning pile of corpses. The Hōjō were so pleased with their 'victory' that they even allowed the enemy storyteller to live.

Meanwhile, Go-Daigo had been captured in Kyoto and exiled to the remote island of Oki. If it had not been for Masashige and Prince Morinaga, the imperial rebellion would certainly have met a premature end with this arrest. But while the two loyalist commanders maintained the royal fight, Go-Daigo smuggled himself onboard a boat and escaped to western Honshu to raise an army. Despite this news, the *bakufu* seemed mainly concerned with destroying the resurrected Masashige, and sent three armies to the samurai's new stronghold of Chihaya Castle. If Akasaka appeared to be a flimsy, makeshift affair built of wood and earth, then Chihaya was by all accounts an impenetrable stone fortress that the Hōjō would never be able to conquer. Masashige would further confound the *bakufu*'s efforts by using every method of siege warfare available, including conducting numerous night attacks, digging large disguised pits along pathways, and leaving perilously perched boulders to drop onto enemy patrols.

The *bakufu* began to worry about Go-Daigo's rising influence in the western Honshu province of Hoki and sent his best commander, Ashikaga Takauji, to deal with him. In the end, the *bakufu's* trust in Takauji turned out to be a terrible mistake. Takauji was related to the Minamoto and, perhaps, had revenge for his cousins in mind when he suddenly decided to defect from the Hōjō and join the imperial side. This was a serious blow for the Hōjō – Takauji was in control of the entire *bakufu* force in the west and a real threat to Kamakura itself. His treachery seemed to have a domino effect, with many clans deciding to swap sides and rally around the emperor. The most important of these was another cousin of the Minamoto, Nitta Yoshisada.

Yoshisada marched on Kamakura with a large army in the name of Go-Daigo, and the subsequent Battle of Kamakura in 1333 became a famous and decisive victory for Yoshisada and the emperor (see page 116). The battle not only marked the demise of the Hōjō regency, but ended Kamakura as the shōgunal capital. In remarkably short time, Go-Daigo had achieved his ultimate goal – the power of the emperor had been restored.

MUROMACHI PERIOD (1338–1573)

With the Hōjō and its capital, Kamakura, destroyed, it must have seemed like the storm clouds had parted for Go-Daigo. Go-Daigo was a great admirer of China, especially its imperial dictatorships, and planned to imitate Japan's neighbour: The subsequent period of history would become known as the Kemmu Restoration. Conversely, his reign as supreme commander of Japan would be both brief and troubled, and it would make the importance of the *bakufu* system that Go-Daigo had destroyed obvious to all.

The first problem concerned the rewards given to the samurai who had helped Go-Daigo to seize power. Traditionally these were titles and land, but Go-Daigo showed himself to be both mean and thoughtless in their distribution. For example, Ashikaga Takauji, the samurai commander who had helped conquer and dispel the mighty Hōjō, assumed that he would be made *shōgun*, but instead Go-Daigo gave the title to one of his sons. Takauji took this as a grave insult, and was further incensed when, in 1335, the emperor ordered him to subdue a small rebel uprising in Kamakura by a rag-tag band of Hōjō supporters.

Takauji responded by considering himself *shōgun* anyway, and decided to consolidate this title by leading an army against Kyoto. Standing in Takauji's way were the imperial heroes Nitta Yoshisada and Kusunoki Masashige; Takauji was defeated and forced to flee to Kyūshū. The samurai clans, on both Kyūshū and Honshu, were now obliged to make their allegiances clear – they were either with Emperor Go-Daigo or with *shōgun* pretender Takauji. As the country divided into two camps, no-one would have predicted that this would lead to a civil war that lasted several centuries. Many samurai clans were unsure which side to back, and so picked the one whose reign would bring the most benefits. Many swapped sides repeatedly, but the one samurai who would retain an obstinate loyalty to the emperor – even when it meant marching to his own death – was Kusunoki Masashige.

It was Masashige's shrewd battle tactics at Akasaka that had prevented the fall of the fortress and the end of Go-Daigo's rebellion while the emperor was exiled on Oki. But this did not seem to have occurred to Go-Daigo when he ordered Masashige to attack Takauji's army, which had landed back on Honshu. Go-Daigo wanted a pitched battle on the shore of the Inland Sea by the Minato River. Masashige strongly disagreed, believing that Takauji should be drawn inland, perhaps even to Mount Hiei, where a battle could be fought from a defensive position, as had been done at Akasaka and Chihaya. Go-Daigo rejected this idea outright and insisted Takauji be met at Minato.

Masashige's willingness to follow Go-Daigo's orders at the cost of his own life made him immortal among samurai. The Battle of Minato River in 1336 was exactly as Masashige predicted – his soldiers were surrounded and overcome by Takauji's army, and he was forced to retreat to a nearby peasant's house with the last handful of his men. The emperor had clearly wanted his samurai to fight to the last man, otherwise he would have allowed Masashige to fight his own style of warfare inland, which had often ended with the commander fleeing to fight another day. In the end, Masashige fulfilled his duty by committing *seppuku*.

NORTHERN AND SOUTHERN COURTS

If the futility of Masashige's martyrdom struck Go-Daigo at any time, it might have been when Takauji's men marched down the streets of Kyoto. Takauji's demands were simple: the emperor would hand over the sacred imperial treasures and abdicate. Go-Daigo did so with great reluctance, but after he had sneaked out of the capital and the official *shōgun* Ashikaga had been crowned the new emperor, the imperial treasures were found to be fake. Go-Daigo had taken the real treasures to his new mountain fortress of Yoshino at Nara, where he continued to call himself the true emperor. So began a period where Japan had two emperors – the southern emperor in Yoshino and the northern emperor in Kyoto.

The effect on the country was entirely predictable: clans flocked to each emperor and went to war. Many learned to play the two courts off against each other for gain, with some fighting mock battles and sending mock reports, so both sides could prove their supposed loyalty. The losers during decades of clan warfare, however, were the peasants, who faced increasingly higher rates of tax and a low quality of life. The Ashikaga shōgunate, on the other hand, went from strength to strength, and in 1392 the most successful of these *shōguns* came to power – Ashikaga Yoshimitsu.

Yoshimitsu was a curious kind of *shōgun* – he was generally liked and actually managed to implement changes of overall benefit to the country. He improved trade with China, built a Zen Buddhist 'Temple of the Golden Pavilion', and resolved the issue of having two emperors. Yoshimitsu did this by convincing both courts to introduce a system of alternate rule. So in 1392, Emperor Go-Komatsu of the northern court became the Emperor of Japan with the promise that the reins would be handed over to the southern court upon his abdication. But the system of alternating emperors was destined for failure, as there would never be an emperor from the southern court.

Yoshimitsu's reign as *shōgun* marked the high water mark for the Ashikaga clan, as the balance of power was now shifting from the capital to the outlying regions. Here, the provincial clans, who had been largely ignored by the *bakufu* in Kyoto, had become increasingly powerful and almost totally autonomous. It was inevitable that, sooner or later, a serious conflict would break out between two or more clans vying for supremacy. When this trouble did indeed come, the Ashikaga, unlike the preceding Kamakura *bakufu*, would prove powerless to prevent it from escalating into an all-out civil war.

The spark which set the tinderbox alight was a succession claim to the Ashikaga shōgunate, disputed by two clans – the Hosokawa and Yamana. The violence began on the streets of Kyoto, with arson attacks and minor skirmishes, but it soon became a serious conflict known as the Ōnin War (1467–77) and all but reduced Kyoto to a pile of burning rubble. After the fighting in Kyoto had played out, it spread to the city's outlying districts, and then into the provinces. After only one year of warfare, the damage was irreparable: the Ashikaga shōgunate collapsed and the country was in the midst of a war in which only the strongest would survive. The heads of these clans were called *daimyo*, or warlords, and were unceasing rivals for power and position. Many clans were simply wiped out, while other smaller factions were forced to join forces to stay alive. The war would become less and less about sides, boundaries or battle lines, and more of an all-out brawl where only the toughest were left standing.

COUNTRY AT WAR

As the capital of Japan burned, so did the notion of hereditary power. Kyoto itself would be rebuilt, but it would never retain its appeal as the cultural hub of courtly charm and civilisation. Nor did a leader of the powerful regional clans need to be an aristocrat to rule. This was the age of country-wide war, or the Sengoku Period, and control went to the most powerful, not those of noble birth. The families of the older orders called the rise of this social meritocracy *gekokujō*, or the 'low overcomes the high'. *Gekokujō* started with the rise of angry mobs of peasants, called *ikki*, and they demonstrated their dissatisfaction by uniting and marching against the rice merchants and moneylenders who had grown rich off peasant labour.

Groups of *ikki* who followed a sect of Buddhism called *Jōdo Shinshū*, or the 'True Pure Land', were known as *Ikkō-ikki*, and they became the first commoners to overthrow a samurai clan and rule in their stead. This took place in the Kaga province in 1488 and the *Ikkō-ikki* retained control there until 1580. They proved to be a military force equal to those of the mighty *daimyo*, which would later become a problem for all involved.

ODA NOBUNAGA

The power of the *Ikkō-ikki* would attract the attention of another underling in the sixteenth century, Oda Nobunaga, who would bring about the end of Japan's civil war and introduce an era of peace. Nobunaga achieved this by utilising a revolutionary new weapon from Europe, which forever changed the way samurai battles were fought.

In 1543 a small fleet of Portuguese merchants had been washed up on the rocky Japanese island of Tanegashima, south of Kyūshū. This shipwreck would have been an unremarkable occurrence in the history of the samurai had it not been for the arquebus muskets the sailors were carrying. The local Tanegashima *daimyo* was so impressed by the firearms that he immediately set his swordsmiths the task of reproducing one. The arquebus would from then on be commonly known in Japan as the *tanegashima*.

The introduction of the arquebus into warfare was highly controversial: here was a weapon that could be fired by a peasant to kill a samurai warrior who had spent his life training for honourable death on the battlefield. On the other hand, it took only days for a peasant foot soldier, or *ashigaru*, to learn to use an arquebus, but years to become an archer.

The bow was a samurai's primary weapon during the early Heian Period, when duels between warriors would begin, and often end, with a mounted archery contest. (Library of Congress)

The genius of the samurai sword was its bi-metallic makeup: a combination of a soft, flexible steel core wrapped in a hard, cutting outer shell. (Shutterstock © Vudhikrai)

Samurai armour typically included a mask with a sinister, grinning mouth, a fake moustache and a helmet adorned with horns, crests and feathers. (Shutterstock © psamtik)

Spared during the onslaught of his family and trained in the theory of warfare, Minamoto Yoritomo was a natural choice to lead an army against the Taira tyrant who had murdered his father. (Shutterstock © Joymsk140)

Opposite: A woodblock print of twelfth-century Prince Yamato Takeru no Mikoto entwined in mortal combat. Artist Taiso Yoshitoshi was famous for his nineteenth-century '*Ukiyo-e*' woodblock artworks, which often depicted brutal and bloody samurai scenes. (Library of Congress)

Minamoto Yoshitsune was the archetypal samurai warrior: young, dashing, loyal and ultimately doomed to failure. His faithful companion, Benkei, who he befriended after an on-bridge duel, followed him to his tragic end. (Shutterstock © Antonio Abrignani)

Opposite top: Kusunoki Masashige's unflinching loyalty to the emperor represented the epitome of the samurai ideal, even when he was being ordered to his certain death. (Shutterstock © Dmitri Ometsinsky)

Opposite bottom: The arquebus was something of a battlefield leveller for the lowly *ashigaru* (foot soldiers), who could be trained to use one within a few days. As such, samurai veterans who had devoted their lives to the art of warfare considered the weapon dishonourable.

のをきく火とをいやま事富をも早くにんのくねぶ
ぜすでも杉をけま小ありうなぬきものしあで

A vivid woodblock print depicting one of the sixteenth-century Kawanakajima battles. Over a period of eleven years, five major battles took place between the Takeda and Uesugi clans. (Library of Congress))

Considered one of the three great unifiers of Japan, Tokugawa Ieyasu was an ambitious warrior with aristocratic blood. He became shogun in 1603 at the age of 60. (Shutterstock © bluehand)

The famous siege of Osaka Castle on 4 December 1614 dispensed with the ideals of honourable warfare, as 100,000 samurai warriors trained their cannons and arquebuses on the castle's royal quarters. (Shutterstock © myfavoritescene)

This woodblock print from a seventeenth-century *ashigaru* fighting manual, the *Zohyo Monogatari*, explains the importance of a full stomach: 'For dying in combat is what we want, but if you die of hunger due to the lack of rice, without fighting the enemy, it would be no better than a tramp's death in the gutter.'

From the seventeenth century, samurai were encouraged to follow peaceful pursuits such as calligraphy, tea ceremonies and painting. Medieval handscrolls celebrated the great samurai battles of yesteryear, while actual duels between warriors were strongly discouraged. (Shutterstock © Maxim Tupikov)

A nineteenth-century woodblock print shows a *rōnin* deflecting arrows with his *naginata*. *Rōnin*, or 'wave men', were masterless samurai, destined to wander aimlessly like the waves in the sea. (Library of Congress)

Woodblock prints, such as this one by eighteenth-century artist Kitagawa Utamaro, reflected Japan's relatively peaceful Edo Period. Unfortunately, Utamaro's career ended in disgrace after he published prints from the banned novel *Hideyoshi and his Five Concubines*, thus insulting the warlord's memory. (Library of Congress)

The first visit of Japanese diplomats to the United States in 1860 received extensive press coverage. *The New York Times* reported that the samurai congregation was 'baffled by and disdainful of many aspects of American culture, and offended by its informality.' (Library of Congress)

In 1868, British diplomat A.B. Mitford was one of the few foreigners to witness a *seppuku* ceremony first hand. His descriptive account recalled the 'hideous noise of the blood throbbing out of the inert heap before us'. (Shutterstock © Antonio Abrignani)

This print from the late nineteenth century may be a retrospective depiction of two warriors at rest. In 1877, as the final act of the samurai's suppression, it became illegal for them to carry swords. (Library of Congress)

Opposite: Saigō Takamori's final charge against a modern army wielding Gatling guns represented the last chapter in the history of the samurai warrior. (Shutterstock © nui7711)

This samurai, sitting for a studio photograph in 1877, would have been unimaginable just thirty years earlier. However, with their caste now abolished, the samurai and their weapons gained a dubious new status as quaint curiosities for visiting foreigners. (Shutterstock)

For a rising young warlord like Nobunaga, the arquebus was simply a new means of ensuring success in battle and he embraced the new technology wholeheartedly.

Nobunaga was born in 1534 to a military governor of the Owari province. By 1560 he had proven his ambition and military prowess by bringing all of Owari under his control and then defeating the neighbouring *daimyo*, Imagawa Yoshimoto. This was no mean feat – Nobunaga was outnumbered five to one by Yoshimoto's army, and the only way to beat him was by catching him unawares with a surprise attack on his camp. So one night after battle, when Yoshimoto's men were celebrating their victories against the new upstart from Owari, Nobunaga and his samurai galloped into the middle of their command camp. Yoshimoto himself was said to have lost his head to two of Nobunaga's mounted samurai as he came out of his tent to quieten down what he assumed were evening revelries. This so-called Battle of Okehazama was important for Nobunaga – it brought his name to the attention of the emperor and signalled the start of an alliance with Tokugawa Ieyasu. Ieyasu was a samurai of the neighbouring Mikawa province who defected from the Yoshimoto side and would be an important samurai figure in the decades which followed. The Battle of Okehazama also marked Nobunaga's association with Toyotomi Hideyoshi, a sandal bearer who went on to become Nobunaga's right-hand man and successor. Nobunaga, Ieyasu and Hideyoshi became the three great unifiers of Japan.

In 1568 Nobunaga moved his headquarters to the city of Gifu and began to support Ashikaga Yoshiaki's bid for the shōgunate. Yoshiaki was the brother of the former *shōgun*, Ashikaga Yoshiteru, who had been assassinated. This was not regarded as headline news, however, as by this time the *shōgun* had become something of a figurehead. Instead, the strongest *daimyo* of the day bullied and manipulated the Ashikaga *shōgun* into doing his bidding, and Nobunaga did not intend to alter this tradition. Nobunaga did not have noble blood, so was not allowed to become *shōgun* himself, but he could certainly be the power behind one. So with the regent system in mind, Nobunaga marched on Kyoto to make Ashikaga Yoshiaki *shōgun* of Japan. Once this had been done, Nobunaga was left free to carry out his plan of taking over every region of Japan in the *shōgun's* name. Consequently, after a few years, Nobunaga no longer needed the *shōgun's* banner and, in 1573, he deposed Yoshiaki. This action, which ended the Ashikaga shōgunate, also officially ended the Muromachi Period.

HOLY WAR

A major hurdle to Nobunaga's plan of bringing every *daimyo* to heel were the *Ikkō-ikki*, who had built temples and strongholds in the strategic locations of Owari, Kaga, Echizen and the provinces surrounding Kyoto. They were a threat through political and economic influence, rather than their military strength. *Ikkō-ikki* strongholds were located across every major trade route, they worked together with almost all of Nobunaga's rivals and would have to be dealt with. Nobunaga's solution was simple – complete elimination.

It is a sign of the *Ikkō-ikki's* growing list of friends that they chose to ally themselves with a much older order of warrior monks – the Enryaku-ji *sōhei* from Mount Hiei. The Enryaku-ji had a well-established history of violent power struggles and Nobunaga decided to make an example of them. In 1570, Nobunaga's samurai marched on Mount Hiei and destroyed everything they found, both buildings and people. The massacre was a signal of Nobunaga's intent and he set about attacking every one of the *Ikkō-ikki's* fortresses. Many of these assaults turned into sieges that lasted for several years before the strongholds were overcome. One example was the fortress of Nagashima on the coast of the Owari province. Nobunaga attacked the stronghold in three different sieges, which included the use of heavy artillery fired from ships. The final siege ended in 1574, when Nobunaga built a wooden palisade around Nagashima and set it alight. Not one of the 20,000 people living at Nagashima escaped the flames.

By 1580 the *Ikkō-ikki* were in retreat, but it was the Battle of Nagashino in 1575 that was arguably Nobunaga's most famous victory. It was here that Nobunaga proved the worth of the arquebus by using three lines of shooters, protected behind a wooden palisade. They would wait until the enemy clan's cavalry were in striking distance and then use their firearms to wipe them out. His samurai were then able to leave the protective fortifications to mop up the survivors with their swords.

Understandably, over time, Nobunaga made many enemies, some of whom were generals from his own army. In 1582, Nobunaga was at the Honnō-ji temple in Kyoto and received word from Toyotomi Hideyoshi that he needed reinforcements; he sent word that General Akechi Mitsuhide should set out to join him. According to legend, upon receiving the order, Akechi said that the enemy was not fighting Hideyoshi, but instead located in Honnō-ji temple. Akechi then gathered a force of samurai and his men to attack the temple and burn it down. It was said that the wounded Nobunaga committed *seppuku* as the flames raged around him.

TOYOTOMI HIDEYOSHI

While Nobunaga had laid the groundwork for the unification of Japan, it was his general and deputy, Toyotomi Hideyoshi, who actually achieved it. Hideyoshi, the sandal-bearing *ashigaru*, had come to Nobunaga's attention during the Battle of Okehazama, where he had branded him 'little monkey' after his physical appearance. However, Hideyoshi proved to be a formidable general and was often described as a 'war-god'.

After avenging Nobunaga's murder by executing Akechi, Hideyoshi set out on a campaign to destroy all of Nobunaga's enemies and bring the country under his control. After a brief conflict with Tokugawa Ieyasu, Ieyasu accepted Hideyoshi as his master and the two went on to conquer the provinces that had not sworn allegiance to Nobunaga.

In 1583, Hideyoshi established himself by building a castle at Osaka and a lavish residence in Kyoto. But like Nobunaga, Hideyoshi was from too lowly a background to become *shōgun*. Instead, he was appointed *kampaku*, or imperial regent, in 1585. Hideyoshi then united the rest of Japan, including the island of Kyūshū, and then, curiously, he passed a law to ensure no mere *gekokujō* like him would ever be able to achieve such a prominent position of authority again.

The legislation required everyone to keep their 'rightful place'. What had prevented this previously was the right of every citizen to bear arms, and Hideyoshi's 'sword hunt' edict therefore made it illegal for anyone except samurai to carry weapons. The law would send any war-mongering *Ikko-ikki* back to their rice paddies and keep the samurai as a aristocratic warrior class. To further ensure these two groups were kept separated, not just militarily but also by wealth and status, they were ordered to live in different parts of towns and villages.

Hideyoshi's subjugation of the island of Kyūshū included the expulsion of the European missionaries. Now Japan was completely unified, Hideyoshi thought it best to remove anything 'un-Japanese'. In fact, the Christians had converted some of the Japanese nobility, which was thought to be the first step in inviting an actual foreign invasion. Hideyoshi's action against foreigners would not end with the missionaries, and by 1590, with all of Japan under his rule, he looked to foreign lands to conquer.

THE KOREAN WAR

Never before in history had Japan attempted to invade a foreign nation, so it is a good indication of Hideyoshi's over-confidence that he planned to invade the largest country in mainland Asia. If Hideyoshi had listened to his advisers, they would have warned of the folly of attacking China. After all, the country was currently under the administration of the mighty Ming Dynasty, the military family who had ousted the ruling Mongols. But this meant little to Hideyoshi, the commander who, after expelling its foreign missionaries, even dared to ask Spain to send warships to aid his invasion. The Spanish reply came in the form of a globe, which clearly marked out the conquered land currently under Spain's dominion and that of Japan's. It is likely this subtle message was lost on Hideyoshi, who, in another impudent move, had invited Korea to join his attack on China. Korea was still a vassal state to imperial China, so Hideyoshi's request was as reckless as it was arrogant. Meanwhile, he prepared a force of nearly 160,000 men to invade the Korean Peninsula.

The first Japanese force landed in the south of Korea in 1592 and proceeded to march northwards, attacking and conquering every fortress that stood in the way. The Korean troops were no match for the Japanese army, which was organised, disciplined and armed with the best weapons ever seen in the East. Yet, while the Japanese were superior on the ground, they were no match for the Korean navy, which included the unfamiliar 'turtleships'. A turtleship was a type of floating tank, covered entirely with iron spikes and carrying up to twenty cannons. As well as being well armed and almost impregnable, the turtleship, with two sails and sixteen oars, had formidable speed and agility in the water.

The Korean navy quickly sank the Japanese ships, breaking the Japanese supply lines. The war soon became a logistical nightmare, as the Japanese samurai reached as far north as Pyongyang and even held the city against an advancing Chinese army. However, with dwindling supplies, Hideyoshi's men were forced to retreat south, closely pursued by the Chinese. The war lasted only a few years and, by 1596, the Japanese had all but pulled out of Korea, leaving a small garrison in the south. Negotiations between the Chinese and Hideyoshi were something of a farce, with lies, deceptions and ridiculous demands from either side. The Japanese translators in particular tried to shield Hideyoshi from what was being demanded of him.

When Hideyoshi learned the Chinese delegates had actually been instructing the Japanese to remove themselves permanently from Korea, the regent lost all control. In an entirely pointless act, Hideyoshi ordered a punitive force of 140,000 samurai back to Korea in 1597. This time, though, the Korean army was ready for him and, together with soldiers sent from China, it defeated the Japanese in 1598. The news was the final straw for Hideyoshi: the 'god of war' was broken by his failure in Korea, and the once great general died later that year at the age of 62.

THE EDO PERIOD (1603–1868)

Hideyoshi's death sparked twenty-four months of civil war as two powerful factions struggled for supreme control. On one side were the Hideyoshi clan supporters: Hideyoshi's former generals, his son, Hideyori, and the regents who ruled on Hideyori's behalf. On the other was Tokugawa Ieyasu, who had served under both Nobunaga and Hideyoshi, but managed to avoid the doomed Korean campaign. Instead, Ieyasu had spent the conflict abroad transferring his lands from his native Mikawa province to the castle town of Edo (later to become Tokyo) on the Kanto plain. Here, he became a successful *daimyo*, maintaining a high level of control over the lands surrounding Edo and administration of the town itself. He made sure the peasantry did not have access to arms, while his castle samurai had direct access to the best supplies and foodstuffs from Edo. In addition, he enlarged his castle and undertook civic engineering works to improve the town's infrastructure. By the time Hideyoshi's disastrous Korean campaign had ended, Ieyasu had made himself the most powerful *daimyo* in Japan with control over its most prosperous domain.

Ieyasu also had higher ambitions than just taking the title of regent. Unlike the commoners Nobunaga and Hideyoshi, Ieyasu had noble Minamoto blood running through his veins. He felt entitled to become *shōgun* and he did not intend to let anybody stand between him and his birthright. So, on 21 October 1600, Ieyasu's army marched out to meet the force still loyal to the late Hideyoshi. The Battle of Sekigahara, fought 50 miles north-east of Kyoto, is often considered one of the greatest fought between samurai in Japanese history (see page 120). Ieyasu won the day at Sekigahara and then destroyed the *daimyo* who had opposed him. Opposition leaders who had not died in battle were encouraged to commit *seppuku*, while those who had fought alongside Ieyasu were rewarded with land and titles.

Ieyasu's victory not only heralded his rise to the rank of *shōgun* in 1603, but led to more than 250 years of Tokugawa rule. It ushered in an age known as the Edo Period, which would last until 1868. Ieyasu played a great political game – he made a public showing of his reverence for the emperor and set up his shōgunate government at Edo. Ieyasu would build on Hideyoshi's reforms that divided the classes along feudal lines, with the samurai becoming a closed caste at the top of the social hierarchy and expected to behave accordingly.

WANDERING SWORDSMEN

As part of his reforms, Ieyasu announced there would be 'no more wars', which in effect made the samurai – warriors who lived and died by the sword – redundant. As a result, Ieyasu started disbanding the clan armies in the provinces, which left many samurai suddenly out of work.

Unemployed samurai without a master to serve were called *rōnin*, or 'wave men', destined to wander aimlessly like the waves in the sea. To counter the rising tide of drifting *rōnin*, Ieyasu reluctantly allowed for samurai to take part in personal duels. So it was the fate of hundreds of thousands of *rōnin* to wander from town to town, looking for suitable opponents to test out their training and talents.

A *rōnin*'s first port of call upon entering a new town was its swordfighting school, many of which sprang up around Japan during the Edo Period. Samurai warriors were handsomely paid to teach at the schools, although it was a risky vocation. If the master of a school lost a duel with a traveling *rōnin*, he would certainly be obliged to resign – that is, if he were still alive.

Samurai duels were to display a warrior's skill and dominance, and were frequently fought to the death. While these duels were supposed to follow the *bushidō* code, many of them were anything but honourable; it was common for a group to lie in wait to ambush a single swordsman. Duelling between *rōnin* became so popular that Ieyasu tried to limit the growing numbers of fatalities by introducing two less harmful duelling swords. One was the *bokken*, made from solid wood, and the other was the *shinai*, made from bamboo slats. Both are still used today in the modern martial art of *kendo*.

There was also another side to the legitimate duels between samurai, which included brawls, street fights and scrapping. Incidents of this entirely dishonourable form of combat grew increasingly common during the Edo Period and, in an attempt to busy the peacetime samurai, Ieyasu encouraged them to learn arts such as calligraphy and poetry, and follow Buddhism. Some samurai gave up their swords to take up previously unthinkable jobs such as bureaucrats, farmers and teachers. Most samurai prayed for an outbreak of war or a local rebellion so they could once again flex their swordfighting muscles. One such opportunity presented itself in 1614, at the end of Tokugawa Ieyasu's reign.

Ieyasu had abdicated his position as *shōgun* in 1605, but ruled from behind the scenes in the time-honoured tradition. His family, however, were never free from the threat of violence as long as Toyotomi Hideyoshi's son, Hideyori, was still alive. Hideyori's large castle at Osaka had become a meeting place for rebels and malcontents, including disaffected *daimyo*, thousands of *rōnin* and a large contingent of Christians. Christian missionaries had already been banned from Japanese soil and practising the religion was heavily discouraged. Now, dispossessed Christians with a grudge had sought out other enemies of Ieyasu and were plotting his downfall.

The following Siege of Osaka began as a series of small Tokugawa victories over outlying towns, before the rebels holed up in Osaka Castle. Then, in 1614, Ieyasu sent a 100,000-strong samurai army armed with arquebuses and cannons to lay siege. Despite being a veteran *daimyo* of dozens of conflicts, Ieyasu practised none of the honourable ideals of samurai warfare. Instead, he trained his cannons at the royal residence rather than the castle walls. Hideyori's mother was cowering inside and the rebel leader had little choice but to sign a peace treaty with Ieyasu. Ieyasu's terms were simple: the *rōnin* inside Osaka would receive a pardon and Hideyori would have to swear not to stage another uprising. What Ieyasu had left out of the treaty – which he signed in his own blood – was that the moat around Osaka Castle would have to be filled in. This was, after all, the Edo Period and Ieyasu had made it clear there would be no more wars. Hideyori did little to protest as the Tokugawa samurai filled in his moat with dirt.

In 1615, news reached Edo that Hideyori was digging out his moat again. This was all the encouragement Ieyasu needed; he raised an army of over 200,000 samurai and marched on Osaka Castle. The armies met on the fields outside Osaka for what would be the last pitched battle of the samurai. The Battle of Tennōji also marked the final change in samurai warfare: there were no called-out challenges or whistling arrows to signal the onset of hostilities; there were not even many horsemen. Instead, lines of foot soldiers armed primarily with arquebuses marched grimly towards one another and clashed in a chaotic and brutal melee. It was perhaps fitting that an arranged battle between two facing armies fought out on the plains would constitute the last samurai battle. This style of warfare, originally borrowed from the Chinese, had been abandoned in the early Heian Period for the one-to-one methods of the Emishi. But there were no more barbarians – only those warriors who at one time had been trained to subdue them – and the samurai were reduced to anonymous slaughter.

The battle won, the Tokugawa samurai surrounded Osaka Castle and set the keep alight, though it is not known if Hideyori and his mother committed *seppuku* before they burned. Hideyori's 8-year-old son, however, was beheaded, as were tens of thousands of *rōnin* residing in the castle. Their heads were then displayed for many miles along the road to Kyoto. In 1616 Tokugawa Ieyasu died, not in battle or as an old man embittered by his failures, but of cancer. Out of the three great unifiers, which included Nobunaga and Hideyoshi, Ieyasu was the leader who secured the longest period of peace. This legacy, however, would make the samurai's role in society a burden and an irrelevance.

FINAL REFORMS AND REVOLTS

After Ieyasu, the Tokugawa shōgunate took further steps to consolidate its control, beginning with the removal of firearms from the local population, which were to be handed over to the *daimyo*. Each *daimyo* was personally appointed by the *shōgun* and had only semi-autonomous rule over his domain. Moreover, it was strictly forbidden for a *daimyo* to mobilise a force outside his borders without the *shōgun*'s permission; and to ensure *daimyos* were not harbouring rebellious thoughts, each was required to have an Edo residence that they inhabited for several months of every year. This costly measure meant *daimyos* had to spend large amounts of time and money travelling and living under the watchful eye of the *shōgun*.

The samurai had already been made a closed caste, but now the social order was frozen into four classes: samurai, peasants, artisans and merchants. It was the job of the peasants, who made up 80 per cent of the country, to feed the samurai, who made up around 6 per cent. While this was hardly fair, the toughest reforms of all would be against Christians and foreigners, and many of these reforms would come about as a direct consequence of the last uprising to take place against a Japanese *shōgun*.

THE SHIMABARA REBELLION

The Shimabara Peninsula was once ruled over by the Arima, a Christian clan who were taken over in 1614 by the Matsukura. *Daimyo* Matsukura Shigeharu was a cruel tyrant and persecutor of Christians, who often set fire to his prisoners or scalded them to death with boiling water. But it was a crippling tax levy that forced the local peasants, Christians, fishermen, craftsmen and *rōnin* of Shimabara into rebellion. The uprising began in 1637 and soon spread across the peninsula, until 37,000 men, women and children occupied the stronghold of Hara Castle. This was no mere peasant rabble – among them were thousands of dispossessed samurai and *ashigaru* who had fought for Ieyasu in the past – and it seemed many of them had also defied the government edict and held on to their arquebuses.

The Tokugawa army sent to attack the castle was made up of over 50,000 samurai, but defending the castle walls were several hundred musketeers, over 500 archers and rock-hurling catapults. Two assaults were made on the fortress and both times the attackers were sent running. The Tokugawa force was a curious mix of older veterans and young, eager samurai who had not yet seen action. Among the veterans was none other than Miyamoto Musashi (see page 11), who was an adviser to the Tokugawa. One legendary moment from the siege has a peasant knocking Musashi from his horse with a carefully aimed stone. Hara Castle held out for six long weeks against the besiegers, which caused major embarrassment to the Tokugawa. Their desperation became evident when a Dutch gunboat used its heavy artillery against the castle walls: a message from the rebels taunted the *shōgun* for needing foreign help and the Dutch boat was duly dismissed.

In the end, the rebels could not defend the castle forever. Their supplies had dwindled and starvation had taken hold when the attacking samurai finally broke through. The resulting scene was one of brutal butchery, as over 125,000 samurai stormed the castle and massacred the 27,000 starving men, woman and children inside.

The cause of the Shimabara Rebellion was clear to the reigning Tokugawa *shōgun*, Iemitsu. For him, Christian ideals brought to Japan by colonising European missionaries had long done harm to the country. Christianity, which had been actively discouraged for some time, was now banned. In addition, Iemitsu made it illegal for any foreigner to enter Japan or any Japanese person to leave, on pain of death. All foreigners, even those Japanese with some foreign blood, were immediately expelled. Japan officially became *sakoku*, a 'locked country', and from 1640 its doors were closed to outsiders. However, a strange loophole in this policy allowed a handful of Dutch merchants access to a small trading port on the artificial island of Dejima, in Nagasaki Harbour, though their influence was kept far from public view.

DECLINE OF THE SAMURAI

Inside the country's closed borders, the peace of the late Edo Period was having dire consequences for those once charged with keeping it. The samurai were still regarded as the aristocratic class and held in the highest esteem, but for the most part they were nobles without money. Samurai were paid a yearly fixed stipend of rice by the *shōgun*, which was often not enough for many to pay their bills. Life in the castle towns that the samurai were legally obliged to inhabit became increasingly expensive from the mid-seventeenth century, as a rising class of merchants and traders, made rich in this time of peace and prosperity, were pushing prices up. Soon, they were the only ones who could afford the high life of restaurants, prostitutes and *kabuki* theatre. Of course, for *daimyo* and high-ranking samurai, many of these temptations were still attainable, but they became inaccessible for low-ranking samurai and *rōnin*.

Many samurai sent their wives out to work or took on jobs themselves, including umbrella-making and farming. Some sold their swords and others their samurai titles. This would have been unthinkable a hundred or even fifty years previously, but so was the idea of a period of national peace. The notion of legions of armed samurai on constant standby for battle was becoming outdated, and actual warfare was replaced by theories on how it should be conducted. *Kendo*, the 'way of the sword', taught students to fight with swords made of wood and bamboo. *Bushidō*, the 'way of the warrior', made its first appearance, too, in the seventeenth century, as did *Hagakure* in the eighteenth century. But these codes and manuals about how to live and die honourably by the sword only disguised the fact that the samurai had become obsolete.

The story of the samurai in nineteenth-century Japan is one of a class of people trying to operate in a world that had no place for them. In its last forty years, the Tokugawa shōgunate was faced with peasant uprisings, samurai bankruptcy and increasing demands from foreign powers for Japan to reopen her doors. In 1853, American gunboats entered Edo Harbour and demanded Japan trade with America. The powerful steamships equipped with shore-pointing guns were daunting symbols of a more advanced civilisation. Two centuries without the influence of foreigners had kept Japan in the technological dark ages, and the *shōgun* had little choice but to accept the American terms.

This decision made the *shōgun* look ineffectual against a foreign invader and further divided the country. There was consensus on one thing, though: a ruler was needed to unify Japan and lead it into a new age, and it seemed most people felt the emperor should fulfil this role. This began the Meiji Restoration, which ironically was first instigated by samurai clan leaders who wanted to keep Japan's borders closed against foreigners. In 1867 the *shōgun* had no choice but to hand its commission back to Emperor Meiji, who then took control of the country.

Those samurai who had opposed the restoration were about to have their worst suspicions confirmed: the emperor abolished the samurai class and discontinued its stipend of rice. The samurai were replaced by a national conscript army and new foreign guns; finally, in 1876, the wearing of swords by samurai was made illegal. This final act enraged Saigō Takamori, the last great samurai in history, who raised an army of samurai against the emperor. He ended his life in a way befitting a warrior – leading a charge against overwhelming enemy numbers, before committing *seppuku* in the face of defeat.

NOTES

1   Sansom, George, *A History of Japan to 1334*

6

Samurai Battles

The battlefield was the great proving ground for the samurai warrior, who spent his whole life in training for combat. Here, a warrior could show off his skill and acumen with a *katana*, and display the *bushidō* virtues of courage and honour.

Early samurai battles were fought according to the traditions of warfare – archery duels, whistling arrows to signal the start of fighting, and *seppuku* in the face of defeat. However, these honourable ideals were only as worthy as the warriors who served them, and many were, of course, devious and dishonest. The codes of *bushidō* were also sometimes contradictory in their messages. Those considered the best warriors were the ones who had put the conditions of warfare to their advantage, so while samurai were encouraged to use the elements – such as fighting with the sun at their back to blind their opponent – they were also expected to conduct a fair fight that was courteous and decent.

As time drew on, the rules of warfare changed. Pitched battles between opposed lines of conscript soldiers were superseded by one-to-one combat and mounted melees during the Heian Period. Then, in the thirteenth century, Kublai Khan's invading warriors from China and Korea showed the samurai how to be cunning and deceptive and generally fight dirty. From then on, the samurai had no qualms about breaking battle conduct and etiquette. The introduction of the arquebus would further affect the rules of conflict and led samurai warfare full circle back to large pitched battles between two facing armies. Here, lines of foot soldiers would fire multiple volleys at their opposite side, making mounted samurai charges increasingly ineffective. This point was confirmed at the last ever samurai battle in 1887, when Saigō Takamori's rebel horsemen were butchered by machine-gun fire. The samurai, trained in the art of honourable warfare and hand-to-hand combat, had become anachronisms.

The three battles that feature in this chapter describe the mechanics and methodology of samurai warfare alongside the heroics and honourable deeds of the protagonists. They are often considered among the most important battles of samurai history, the results of which had large and often devastating consequences for the country.

THE BATTLE OF KURIKARA

The Battle of Kurikara was the largest battle yet fought between two samurai armies and certainly the greatest encounter of the Genpei War (1180–85), which was played out between the two most powerful clans of Japan at that time – the Minamoto, also known as the *Genji*, and the Taira, often called the *Heike*. The Taira had recently come to dominate the imperial court through their leader and regent Taira Kiyomori, a power-mad megalomaniac whose greatest ambition after seizing the throne was to destroy the Minamoto. Kiyomori had died before these dreams came true, but his parting words were 'make haste and slay Yoritomo and cut off his head and lay it before my tomb'.

Yoritomo was the unofficial leader of the Minamoto clan, although his right to rule came under attack from his cousin, Yoshinaka. The trouble between the two came to a head in March 1183 when Yorimoto marched his army out to meet Yoshinaka's. However, the battle was not fated to take place: Yoshinaka convinced his cousin that they should combine and attack their sworn enemies, the Taira, rather than each other. Yoshinaka sealed the agreement by sending his son back to Yoritomo's headquarters in Kamakura as a hostage. Yoshinaka then rode out to fight the Taira, who were on the march from the capital city of Kyoto.

The Taira were also internally divided and had recently suffered a great loss of face during their first battle with the Minamoto. The night before, the Taira camp had become spooked by a dispersing flock of water fowl from a nearby lake and fled. Koremori, the commander in charge of this shameful retreat, was now leading the Taira force toward Yoshinaka in the north. Koremori's dubious leadership ability was again underlined only days after the army left Kyoto. Many of his men had already deserted and those remaining had completely run out of food. According to the *Heike Monogatari*, the Taira army therefore 'began to seize and appropriate anything they wanted from the estates and houses that lay by the way, not sparing even the government property … the inhabitants of these places could not endure it and fled to the mountains'.

Some of the Taira's high-ranking samurai then decided to take a break, one of them 'wishing to calm his mind in the midst of these alarms and disorder'.[1] So they rowed out to the centre of a nearby lake to take in the scenery and compose poetry. Although most of the Taira force was recorded as continuing on its march, the scene is an interesting insight into the psyche of the Taira: both warring clans were originally of noble blood, but the Taira were renowned as the provincial clan of culture and refinement, whereas the Minamoto were often described as coarse and uncouth. Their differing appreciation for tradition and ceremony – especially the honourable ideals of samurai warfare – would be a contributing factor to the conflict that followed.

BANNERS AND BOVINES

The *Heike Monogatari* estimates the Taira army to have been 100,000 men as it approached the mountain pass of Kurikara. The number in reality

113

would have been far less, but it was probably in the tens of thousands. As this mighty army made its way slowly up the Kurikara Pass, it glimpsed the encampment of a far bigger force, or so they thought. Yoshinaka had assumed the Taira would attack with large numbers, so it was best, Yoshinaka mused in the *Heike Monogatari*, to play the Taira at their own game: 'If a large force is menaced by a larger one it will feel in danger of being surrounded … and so, fearing to be surrounded if they [the Taira] move forward, they will consider it the safest plan to stop for a while and rest their horses.' To reinforce the illusion of larger numbers, Yoshinaka set up thirty white banners on the nearby Kurosaka Hill. As the Taira reached the top of the Kurikara Pass, they looked down to see the Minamoto flags and, as predicted, decided to make camp and rest their horses rather than risk being flanked during their descent.

Seeing his ruse had worked, Yoshinaka split his 40,000-strong army into three parts: one group would move up and around the Taira camp, ready to attack it from the rear; the second group would be sent to stand in position below the pass; and Yoshinaka would keep the third group with him on the nearby Kurosaka Hill. The main obstacle to the plan was how to conduct these manoeuvres undetected by the Taira, and Yoshinaka's solution was a classically simple piece of military genius – he created a diversion. He did so by engaging the Taira in a traditional samurai battle, one that would feature whistling arrows, the calling out of one samurai to a potential opponent, and bouts of one-to-one combat. While one of Yoshinaka's detachments kept the Taira fighting, his other groups would move into position.

The plan was a brilliant success. Perhaps the Taira were even flattered that a barbarous lout such as Yoshinaka would think to fight a battle according to the time-honoured customs of their samurai forefathers. So it was that, on the morning on 2 June 1183, the full Taira army stood facing one third of the Minamoto army, with around 300m separating them. The Minamoto were first to act, as fifteen of their samurai walked forward and each sent a whistling arrow into the air. In reply, fifteen Taira samurai stepped forward and loosened their own whistling arrows. The Minamoto responded by sending out thirty more samurai to fire arrows, and the Taira did the same. This continued until a hundred men had stepped out on either side and begun hand-to-hand combat. This was an effective way to waste time and the Minamoto did not send out any more samurai to challenge the Taira. Instead, the fighting continued until dusk, with the two opposing armies looking on.

It was at this time that Yoshinaka's first detachment attacked the Taira's rear, beating on their quivers and shouting war cries. Then the second Minamoto group charged down from the slopes above the Taira. But it was Yoshinaka's final tactic that sealed the fate of the now-surrounded enemy. Perhaps the idea had come from the water fowl that had so frightened the Taira previously, but this time it was not birds but a herd of bulls that Yoshinaka let loose on his enemy. To make the spectacle even more terrifying, the Minamoto had tied a flaming torch between the horns of each beast, all of which were now charging down the narrow Kurikara Pass towards the Taira. Many of these men were knocked off the path and into the rocky ravine below, while others simply jumped to their death. The *Heike Monogatari* describes the scene:

> The Genji rushed to the attack on both front and rear, and though many adjured their fellows to come back and not to disgrace themselves by flight, when once panic seizes a great army it is not of easy to stop it, so the Heike stampeded in a pell-mell flight into the valley of Kurikara. As those behind could not see those in front, they thought there must be a road at the bottom of the valley, and so the whole army went down one after another, son after father, brother after brother and retainer after lord, horses and men falling on top of one another and piling up in heaps upon heaps. Thus did some seventy thousand horsemen of the Heike perish, buried in this one deep valley: the mountain streams ran with their blood and the mound of corpses was like a small hill; and in this valley, it is said, there can be seen the marks of arrows and swords even to this day.[2]

The Battle of Kurikara ended with Yoshinaka taking the decisive victory, although it was cunning rather than large numbers which had won the day. Kurikara would go down in the annals as the first major victory for the Minamoto, and signalled the start of the Taira clan's descent to final destruction.

THE BATTLE OF KAMAKURA

After the Battle of Kurikara and the end of the Genpei War, the Minamoto had emerged as the clear victors. They had not only destroyed the Taira's forces in a long series of battles, but almost annihilated the clan itself. The commanders had been Yoshinaka and Yoshitsune, the cousin and brother of clan leader, Yoritomo, respectively. But there would be no triumphant parade for these samurai leaders back at the Minamoto headquarters of Kamakura. Instead, Yoritomo had both men killed, which left the way open for his unhindered rise to power. In 1192 Yoritomo was awarded the title of *shōgun*, although the position was short-lived – Yoritomo died in 1199 in a riding accident and Minamoto control diminished thereafter. Instead, the Hōjō clan would take over, ruling as shōgunal regents for over a century.

In 1318 the Hōjō regent was Takatoki, a notoriously debauched and weak-willed leader who preferred dog-fighting to protecting the imperial interests. However, this was actually fortunate for the emperor at the time, Go-Daigo, whose obsession was to do away with *shōguns* and regents and restore absolute control to the imperial throne. He set about doing so by secretly wooing sympathetic clans. It took Takatoki some years to act on intelligence about the emperor's plan to usurp his authority, and in 1333 he sent an army to the imperial capital in Kyoto.

This army was led by Ashikaga Takauji, who decided at some point on the march to Kyoto that he had more to gain by serving the emperor and defected to the imperial side. It did not take long for news to reach Takatoki that Takauji had killed the Hōjō representative in Kyoto and burned his headquarters to the ground. Worse news was to come when the Hōjō at Kamakura learned that a samurai army had been dispatched by the emperor to wipe them out. The force was being led by Nitta Yoshisada, a Minamoto relative who had the complete backing of the

116

emperor. This was clearly intended to be an all-or-nothing battle, the winner of which would leave either the emperor or the Hōjō regent in control of the country.

Yoshisada was riding towards Kamakura with his ever-expanding army 'when tidings of Yoshisada's victories were proclaimed abroad; like clouds or mist the warriors of the eight eastern provinces joined themselves to him'.[3] By the time this army was making its approach to Kamakura, it was said to number 800,000. In reality, the army would have been around a tenth of this number, but it would certainly have outnumbered the defending Kamakura force, which the *Taiheiki* records as numbering 150,000.

PRAYER, PASSES AND DRAGON-GODS

Yoshisada divided his force into three groups, and each one was to concentrate its attack on three of the seven narrow passes leading into Kamakura. Kamakura was in a valley surrounded on three sides by mountains and the sea at its front. The mountain passes into the valley were steep, narrow and, in parts, almost completely covered by forest, although each was wide enough to accommodate a horse. On 18 May 1331, Yoshisada chose to send his three detachments east and north to the Gokurakuji Pass, the Kewaizaka Pass and the Kobukurozaka Pass. The *Taiheiki* describes the life and death drama that took place at each of three passes:

> The attackers pressed forward with fresh men, time after time, so great were their numbers; the defenders held stubbornly in many engagements, so vital were their strongholds … Assuredly was this a battle to decide great things, one such as would make it known to generations to come whether those who contended together were brave or cowardly. When a son was stricken, his father did not minister to him, but rode over his body to attack the enemy in front; when a lord was shot down from his horse by an arrow, his retainer did not raise him up, but mounted onto the horse and galloped forward. Some grappled with enemies to the end; some exchanged sword-thrusts and died together with their foes. It was

impossible to know when the battle might cease, so valiant was the spirit of those warriors.[4]

After much fierce combat, none of Yoshisada's three columns had broken through. That night Yoshisada took a contingent of men to a high point to survey the ground around the Gokurakuji Pass; this pass had particularly strong fortifications, with the way being nearly blocked by large wooden shields. Yoshisada could make out the torches of the Hōjō camp below, where thousands of samurai were awaiting another assault in the morning. But south of the Gokurakuji Pass was the Inamura Cape, a small peninsula that protected Kamakura from the adjourning bay. Unfortunately, there was no beach around the cape to enter Kamakura, only sheer cliffs. The edge of the cape was also closely watched by Hōjō ships, whose archers kept a keen lookout for a seaward attack.

Only divine intervention would be able to help the emperor's commander and, with this in mind, Yoshisada took off his helmet and prayed to the dragon-gods of the sea. Immediately, according to the *Taiheiki*, Yoshisada's prayers were answered: 'Suddenly for more than two thousand yards the waters ebbed away from Inamura Cape, where for the first time a broad flat beach appeared.'[5]

For the more cynically minded, the passage could be interpreted to mean that Yoshisada's prayer happened to coincide with the tide rolling back, therefore exposing an otherwise unseen strip of beach. Either way, this was the break the imperial commander had been looking for.

THE FALL OF KAMAKURA

It took only hours for the imperial samurai to enter Kamakura and engage the Hōjō in a ferocious battle on the streets. As the warriors pushed further into the city's heart, they set fire to anything that would burn and Kamakura soon became a chaotic inferno:

> Entering clamorously beneath the fierce flames, the warriors of the Genji everywhere shot the bewildered enemy with their arrows, cut them down

with their swords, grappled with them, and stabbed them. They captured prisoners, took spoils, and chased women and children wandering lost in the smoke, causing them to flee into fires or tumble down to the bottoms of ditches.[6]

As the battle wore on, the Hōjō defence became one of heroic last charges and samurai suicides. At several points, Hōjō warriors were actually called away from holding a blade to their abdomens to take as many of the enemy with them as possible: 'Those who grappled fell down together to the ground, where some took heads and the heads of some were taken. The sky was darkened with rising dust; the earth was clotted with sweat and blood.'[7] There are examples of Hōjō valour, fighting for death and glory in an attempt to uphold the samurai traditions of warfare. However, the *Taiheiki* chronicle ends with a grisly account of group suicide. The text vividly paints the *seppuku* with poetic flourishes: last sentiments are shared between parents who then stab their babies; death poems are written in blood on temple pillars; stomachs are slashed open and innards pulled out. Other Hōjō samurai are required to help their master by beheading him at the pivotal *seppuku* moment and then burning his house so his head cannot be taken as a trophy. Then, in the true samurai tradition of following their master unto death, the lord's men follow suit:

> The retainers who were left behind ran out to the middle gate, crying aloud, 'Our lord has killed himself! Let all loyal men accompany him!' Then these twenty lighted a fire in the mansion, quickly lined up together in the smoke, and cut their bellies. And not willing to be outdone, three hundred other warriors cut their bellies and leapt into the consuming flames.[8]

The scene was repeated in buildings around the city as it was overrun with the imperial samurai. The result was the largest mass suicide in samurai history:

> Thereafter, a fire was lighted in the hall, wherefrom fierce flames leapt up and black smoke darkened the sky. When the warriors in the courtyard and before

the gate beheld that fire, some among them cut their bellies and ran into the flames, while others smote one another with their swords and fell down together in a heap, fathers, sons, and brothers. As a great river was the rushing of their blood; as on a burial field were their dead bodies laid everywhere in piles! Although the bodies of these disappeared in the flames, later it was known that more than eight hundred and seventy men perished in this one place.[9]

The civilian dead were thrown into pits and mass graves, while samurai corpses were stored away in caves and separate burial holes. While many of these samurai were buried without their heads, Yoshisada's men made sure that the proper funerary honours were bestowed upon their enemy counterparts.

The destruction of Kamakura spelled the end of the Hōjō and the clan's regency, and marked the restoration of the emperor. However, the imperial return to power would be short and turbulent, and within a few years a new *shōgun* would be back in control.

THE BATTLE OF SEKIGAHARA

The Battle of Sekigahara in 1600 was fought between two of the largest samurai armies ever assembled and is one of the most celebrated battles in Japanese history. Sekigahara was a pitched battle which incorporated the new technology of arquebuses alongside the more traditional horsemen, archers and foot soldiers. However, the one-day conflict is perhaps less interesting for the mechanics of its warfare than it is for the dramatic themes of loyalty, treachery and chance that were played out in the fog and mud of the battlefield.

Japan was undergoing periodic unification by warlords and regents at this time. The first of these unifying regents was Oda Nobunaga, who was followed by Toyotomi Hideyoshi. Hideyoshi had been so successful in uniting Japan's warring clans that he turned his attentions to new campaigns overseas. His plan had been to invade China, but two disastrous campaigns at the end of the thirteenth century ended in failure and the unwarranted destruction of Korea. This failure broke Hideyoshi's spirit and the regent died a bitter man in 1598. His death was to throw Japan back into a state of civil war which set the process of unification back two more years.

The problem lay in Hideyoshi's successor, his 5-year-old son, Hideyori. Five regents were appointed to govern by committee in Hideyori's stead until he became old enough to rule, but tensions among the regents became quickly evident and clandestine alliances were formed. Two factions emerged after one of the regents died: on one side were the Hideyoshi clan supporters, led by Ishida Mitsunari and including the Korean veterans Kobayakawa Hideaki and Shimazu Yoshihiro; on the other side were Tokugawa Ieyasu, the most powerful *daimyo* in Japan, and his allies.

Ishida Mitsunari and Tokugawa Ieyasu could not have been more different. Ishida was a samurai bureaucrat and a prudent military organiser, who had won favour with Hideyoshi and been made *daimyo* of Sawayama. Ishida's loyalty to Hideyoshi had been absolute and was transferred to the dead regent's son, Hideyori. Opposing Ishida was Tokugawa Ieyasu, a highly esteemed veteran general who had fought under Nobunaga and Toyotomi Hideyoshi. Ieyasu had managed to avoid taking part in Hideyoshi's conflict in Korea and, instead, became the *daimyo* of Edo province. Ieyasu not only commanded respect, but he was also rich and led one of the largest samurai armies in the country. Unlike Nobunaga and Hideyoshi, who were of peasant stock, Ieyasu was related to the aristocratic Minamoto clan, meaning that he did not have to settle for the title of regent as Nobunaga and Hideyoshi were forced to do – he could become *shōgun*. And so with the battle lines drawn, Ieyasu set out to achieve his ultimate goal.

After a series of sieges and skirmishes in early 1600, the two great armies met at Sekigahara, a narrow pass located between two plains at Lake Biwa and Nagoya. Leading the 82,000-strong western army was Ishida and, opposite him, the 89,000-strong eastern army was led by Ieyasu. Firearms were estimated to have been carried by around 10 per cent of the samurai at Sekigahara, including over 20,000 arquebuses.

Some of this weaponry had come from a Dutch merchant boat, the *Liefde*, shipwrecked off the coast of Kyūshū. Ieyasu had seized the cargo from the *Liefde*, which included nineteen bronze cannons and 500 muskets, plus gunpowder and ammunition.

The night of 20 October 1600 was one of unceasing torrential rain, which fell most heavily on Ishida's men who were digging trenches in the Sekigahara Valley. On one of the hills above the valley was Kobayakawa Hideaki and his army, and on the hill opposite was the Shimazu clan and Ishida himself. Ishida had a simple plan for battle: once his samurai had engaged Ieyasu's men in the valley, Ishida would light a fire to signal Hideaki, who would swoop down from above. However, behind the scenes, Hideaki had also been in talks with Ieyasu and had agreed to defect at the pivotal moment.

BATTLE LINES AND DEFECTIONS

On the morning of 21 October the rain had given place to a fog so thick that the samurai in the valley could hear but not see their enemy. There were some confused clashes and shots fired, but the valley commanders quickly pulled their men back until the sun had broken through and the fog lifted. The colourful banners and gleaming armour of the two enemy armies dazzled their generals looking down from above. Both sides now engaged: arquebuses were fired and mounted charges began, but the rains had made a quagmire of the battlefield, and the close-hand fighting turned into a muddy and messy melee.

Part of the eastern army was ordered towards the hill occupied by Ishida in an attempt to take out the western army leader and bring about a decisive result. Ishida responded by using his large artillery at the approaching enemy, which mostly only served to add to the noise, smoke and confused conditions in the valley below. Here the samurai were wading though a knee-deep ooze to hack at each other, and Ishida decided the time was right to signal Hideaki to enter the fray. But when he saw the signal fire, Hideaki seemed not to move, and instead sat on his horse watching the battle below. Two of the western army commanders in the valley, Konishi Yukinaga and Ōtani Yoshitsugu, were aghast at Hideaki's inaction, which was surely going to seal their defeat. Konishi sent a messenger up to Hideaki demanding he do his duty, but the samurai leader remained still. Yoshitsugu, a leper who was leading from the comfort of a palanquin, suspected the worst and ordered his samurai to ready their muskets against a potential attack by their ally Hideaki.

Ishida and his commanders were not the only ones waiting for Hideaki's charge, and Ieyasu was also watching impatiently for the samurai to defect. No-one will ever know what was going through Hideaki's mind that day; he had promised his sword to both armies and he now had the power to win the day for either side. His hesitation may have signalled fear, indecision or unwillingness to send his men into battle prematurely, but it was Ieyasu who took the biggest risk of the day to spur the samurai into action. He sent a small contingent of musketeers to fire on Hideaki's position. Incredibly, this had the desired effect: Hideaki issued the command for his warriors to attack their own side and his army of 15,000 samurai charged down the hill towards Yoshitsugu's line. Yoshitsugu's men had been readied for this moment and trained their arquebuses towards the oncoming charge, picking off hundreds of Hideaki's advancing samurai. Nevertheless, their number was too great to hold off, and, as the Yoshitsugu line was broken, Yoshitsugu committed *seppuku*.

Konishi Yukinaga and his men, also caught up in Hideaki's treacherous attack, fought to the death. As a result, the day had turned and many other samurai decided to switch sides. One clan who may have been hesitating were the Shimazu, who, despite a number of direct orders from Ishida, had refused to join the fight. Now the Shimazu were in danger of being overrun by the approaching eastern army, and, instead of defecting to them, Shimazu Yoshihiro ordered his men to retreat. This they did, calling out news of Hideaki's treachery to other western army clans as they rode, causing many of them to switch sides as a result.

By early afternoon the battle was over and Ieyasu was sitting on his stool surveying the large numbers of enemy samurai heads being brought to him in the usual manner. Ishida managed to escape from the battleground, but was hunted down and decapitated some days later,

123

while his allies were either executed, invited to commit *seppuku*, or stripped of their titles and domains. Those who had supported Ieyasu, and even those who had defected to him on the battlefield, were rewarded with land and titles.

Ieyasu won the title of *shōgun* and laid the foundations for over 250 years of peace in Japan, commonly known as the Edo Period. This period would end in 1868 with Japan's forced re-entry into contact with other countries and the abolition of the samurai. So while the Battle of Sekigahara would win Tokugawa Ieyasu the coveted prize of *shōgun* ruler, it would also mark the beginning of the samurai's ultimate demise.

NOTES

1 *Taiheiki: A Chronicle of Medieval Japan*
2 *Heike Monogatari*
3 *Taiheiki*
4 *Heike Monogatari*
5 *Taiheiki*
6 Ibid.
7 Ibid.
8 Ibid.
9 Ibid.

7

The Warriors

The great heroes of the samurai age did not have to wait long to be immortalised, as their epic exploits were recounted in artworks, poems, plays and books. Often these warriors appeared to be *bushidō* purists: they were refined, educated gentlemen; honourable, stoic, honest and unwaveringly courageous on the battlefield. Modern portrayals tend to take the same view, emphasising the warrior's martial prowess and accomplishments in war. Like any military hero, a samurai was expected to be an indomitable figure in battle, a respected champion and a great leader of men. But it is the warrior's relationship with *bushidō*, both on the battlefield and off it, that makes up one of the great contradictions of the samurai.

In fact, many successful samurai commanders were anything but refined and educated. For instance, although originally born of royal blood, the Minamoto clan held a well-founded reputation for being uncouth, uncultured and unwashed. Minamoto Yoshinaka astounded the genteel folk of Kyoto when, as general and liberator, he did not even know how to dismount correctly from a carriage. He further confounded matters by insulting courtiers, breaking court protocol and dressing like a vagrant.

There were also no guarantees that those cultivated samurai who were well versed in etiquette and tradition would actually behave well. Honour was one of the key virtues of the *bushidō* code, but it often gave way to ambition and self-interest. Loyalty was another elusive virtue; in theory it was the pre-eminent quality of the samurai that was prized above all else. Any worthy warrior would follow his master into death or lay down his life for him, but loyalty to *whom*, or *what*, was another question. The emperor was considered to be the most important man in Japan, until the provincial clans decided they did not want to serve him. He was then replaced with a *shōgun* or a regent. But *shōguns*, too, were capable of disloyalty: samurai would follow their *shōgun* or clan leader to the ends of the earth, but their fidelity was often rewarded with death or betrayal. Loyalty to one's clan was considered essential, but brothers would not hesitate to kill each other to better their own position.

The stories of the greatest samurai heroes are parables of loyalty to one's clan, one's emperor, one's master and oneself, but they often don't reflect the darker reality. It is the complex relationship with this topmost *bushidō* virtue that defined the legacies of these samurai and often triggered their demise.

MINAMOTO YOSHIIE

Minamoto Yoshiie is often considered the quintessential samurai warrior: he was a formidable soldier, a cultured and respected leader, and his memory lasted well beyond the end of the samurai era. He was also the first samurai warlord to openly show dissent towards the emperor, which paved the way for centuries of shōgunal rule.

Yoshiie was born in 1039 to Yoriyoshi, the governor ordered to suppress a rebellion among the Abe clan of the Dewa province in northern Honshu. The Abe had been charged with controlling the local Emishi of this outlying region and, over time, the clan had become rich, powerful and almost completely autonomous. The clan later fell under the full imperial gaze when it refused to pay taxes and then took arms against the Fujiwara tax collectors.

The resulting campaign between Yoriyoshi and the Abe became known as the Early Nine Years' War, and Yoshiie followed his father into every battle. His accuracy with a bow from horseback was legendary – he was said to gallop like the wind and make every arrow inflict a mortal wound. Yoshiie distinguished himself in the Battle of Kawasaki in 1057 by fighting off an Abe rearguard attack as the Minamoto retreated through a snowstorm. His actions in the battle earned the young samurai the name *Hachimantaro*, 'the God of War', but it was in a future encounter with the Abe where Yoshiie would exhibit the loyalty and honour expected of a true samurai warrior.

A Minamoto attack on Koromo Castle had forced the Abe leader, Sadato, and his bodyguard to flee on horseback. Yoshiie galloped after Sadato, who became separated from his retainers and took refuge in a nearby forest. Sadato was wounded and tried to escape his pursuer, but Yoshiie called out: 'Wasn't he ashamed to turn his back on his enemy who had a message for him?' Sadato turned to face Yoshiie, who, instead of attacking, recited a verse from a poem: 'The warps of your robe have come undone', meaning that Koromo Castle had been destroyed. To this Sadato called back another verse from the same poem: 'Over the years its threads became tangled, and this pains me.' And with this gentlemanly exchange, Yoshiie turned and let the enemy leader go, deeming this the honourable course of action.

Yoshiie eventually defeated the Abe and was made Governor of Mutsu as a reward. In 1083 the emperor called on him to quell another uprising, which, in turn, led to another clan war. The conflict initially involved infighting among clans of the Kiyowara family, who had helped the Minamoto defeat the Abe during the Early Nine Years' War. After an initial investigation into the rebellion, Yoshiie decided to settle the matter through force and attacked the rogue Kiyowara clans. This action culminated in the Later Three Years' War, which did not have the approval of the imperial court. Nevertheless, the war created another legendary Yoshiie story.

One of the first samurai celebrated as displaying *bushidō* virtues, Yoshiie had educated himself in the philosophy and craft of warfare. One day, as he rode at the head of his army, Yoshiie noticed a flock of birds rise suddenly from a field in front of him. Remembering a Chinese book on strategy, Yoshiie realised the birds may have exposed an ambush. The commander then ordered his men to surround the field and create an ambush of their own. Sure enough, a group of enemy warriors were found lying hidden in wait and were quickly executed.

By the end of the war, Yoshiie had defeated the rogue Kiyowara clans and strengthened the Minamoto powerbase in the north. Yet, although Yoshiie had the love and devotion of his men, the imperial court was not similarly enamoured. It had disapproved of Yoshiie's approach to subduing the Kiyowara rebellion and refused his request to execute the rebel leaders. The court also refused to pay Yoshiie's men because the war had not been commissioned by the emperor.

Outraged by this, Yoshiie killed the enemy leaders anyway and discarded their heads in a ditch: an unthinkable insult to the families of the dead samurai. He then paid his men from his own pocket and escaped reprisals in the capital by riding to his castle in the north. The imperial court was furious and immediately removed his governorship, but Yoshiie had expected this and did not appear disturbed. He had secured great power and position for the Minamoto clan and had cemented his reputation as a formidable samurai leader. It was also unlikely that the emperor would ever stage a military attack against Yoshiie. After all, this was the commander the emperor once called upon to protect the capital from attack by the Kyoto warrior monks. The attack was never made, but the move had shown the emperor felt that both the warrior monks and the Minamoto were greater military forces than the Fujiwara charged with protecting the imperial court.

Yoshiie and other provincial samurai leaders began to pose a great threat to the court, though oddly, as the clans' influence grew, the court's interest in their activities waned. This would, in turn, enable the rise of powerful samurai armies and create the *shōgun* era of the twelfth century. Minamoto Yoshiie died in 1106 before this happened, but his legend provided a benchmark for the *shōgun* that followed, showing the might and will of the samurai to be greater than that of the emperor.

MINAMOTO YOSHITSUNE

Minamoto Yoshitsune is the samurai hero of the Genpei War and the subject of countless books, plays and poems. Like his predecessor, Yoshiie, Yoshitsune is something of a samurai archetype: refined, educated and trained in the arts of war; young, dashing and successful with women; loyal and self-sacrificing. In the end, however, he was doomed to failure. It is this last point which appears to make Yoshitsune such an attractive historical figure in Japan. Despite his great military deeds and blind devotion to his clan leader and brother, Yoritomo, Yoshitsune's destiny is to be condemned as an outlaw. The fatalistic appeal of the lone, ostracised samurai is an often repeated and celebrated theme in Japanese legend and folklore.

Yoshitsune was born in 1159 to Minamoto Yoshitomo, one of the leading protagonists of the ill-fated Heiji Rebellion. Unlike his father and brother, Yoshihira, Yoshitsune was spared decapitation following the rebellion and was sent to be raised in a monastery. Despite this, Yoshitsune found a way of training himself in the samurai arts. In the many accounts of his life, some record the young Minamoto sneaking away to practise alone in secret; others describe Yoshitsune being tutored by the '*tengu*' demons that dwelled in a nearby forest. Either way, Yoshitsune became an exceptional warrior by the time he was a young man, and soon left the monastery for the Minamoto lands in the north.

Yoshitsune's travels north are full of the colourful stories so often associated with wandering samurai swordsmen. He fights off several bands of bandits, makes various friends and companions, and has his first encounter with a woman, a Taira lord's daughter. However, the anecdote is less about the pleasures of the flesh than the academic pursuit of knowledge. The girl's father was the owner of a Chinese manual on war, which Yoshitsune found and studied during the several nights of his assignations.

Yoshitsune's most famous meeting was with a warrior monk who would become his loyal comrade. This was Benkei, a 6ft 6in man with wild hair and godlike strength. Yoshitsune met Benkei at the Gojō Bridge in Kyoto, where the monk had taken a vow to disarm 1,000 warriors as they tried to cross. As luck would have it, 999 swords had already been collected when Yoshitsune stepped onto the bridge. Of course, the young samurai would not become Benkei's thousandth victim and, instead, the giant monk found himself disarmed and defeated. Benkei was obliged to pledge his lifelong allegiance to Yoshitsune, a promise he kept.

In 1180 Yoshitsune began working for his brother, Yoritomo, as a Minamoto commander fighting the Taira in the Genpei War. However, his first foe in battle was his cousin Yoshinaka. Yoshinaka had been overwhelmingly successful in his battles with the Taira, but would not accept Yoritomo as Minamoto clan leader and seized control of Kyoto for himself. Yoshitsune successfully led an army against Yoshinaka's samurai at the second Battle of Uji Bridge and ousted his cousin from the capital.

Yoshitsune was then charged with crushing what was left of the Taira clan, which he carried out in a series of battles between 1184 and 1185. In the end the Taira were completely destroyed and, for a brief moment, Yoshitsune was the victorious commander who won the Genpei War for the Minamoto. But while he expected a triumphant return to the Minamoto base in Kamakura, he was sadly disappointed: the heroic general was soon to be made an outlaw.

THE TIDE TURNS

Yoshitsune's problems had started some months before at the Battle of Yashima. Here, he had clashed with one of his generals, Kajiwara Kagetoki, who suggested the Minamoto ships be equipped with reverse-facing oars to enable a retreat if necessary. The two commanders had nearly come to blows over the disagreement and Kagetoki had written to Yoritomo to give a full and detailed account of his brother's command, likening him to a 'wild-boar warrior'. There would be a further incident at the final battle of the war at Dannoura, when Kagetoki asked to lead the Minamoto navy:

> On that day the Hogwan [Yoshitsune] and Kajiwara were on the point of open warfare with each other. Kajiwara came to the Hogwan and requested that he might be allowed to lead the Genji fleet. 'Certainly,' replied Yoshitsune, 'if I am prevented.' 'That is not proper,' answered Kajiwara, 'for your lordship is Commander-in-Chief.' 'By no means,' replied the Hogwan, 'Yoritomo is the real Commander-in-Chief, and I am only a Marshal of the forces, so I am equal in rank to you.' 'H'm,' grumbled Kajiwara, disappointed of his expectation of leading the army, 'his lordship is not naturally suited to lead warriors.' 'Your lordship seems to me the biggest fool in Nippon,' retorted Yoshitsune, laying his hand on his sword hilt. 'This to me!' exclaimed Kajiwara, also laying his hand on his sword, 'I, who have no other lord but Kamakura Dono! [Yoritomo].'[1]

The two were pulled apart before they were able to harm each other, but the real damage had been done as 'from that time Kagetoki nursed his enmity against Yoshitsune, and spoke evil of him, so that at last he got him put to death, as is elsewhere recorded'.[2]

Kagetoki's reports about Yoshitsune came as music to Yoritomo's ears, as it gave the jealous and suspicious Minamoto leader the grounds to destroy his brother. So when Yoshitsune returned to Kyoto as the triumphant general, he found himself accused by Yoritomo of lazy and reckless leadership, which had placed the lives of his men in unnecessary peril. A stunned Yoshitsune was not granted an audience with Yoritomo to defend himself, and was even banned from entering Kamakura at all. The shocked Minamoto wrote a letter and gave it to one of his estranged brother's retainers, in the hope it would be received by him:

> With the deepest respect Minamoto Yoshitsune pleads his cause. Having been appointed to represent your lordship, I have successfully fulfilled the

Imperial Edict in subduing the enemies of the Throne and wiping out our former disgrace. Far from receiving any reward for these deeds, on account of some malignant slander all my great merit has been forgotten, and I have been blamed where I have committed no crime. Though my great achievements are known to all, yet I am thus rebuffed and left here many days to weep bitter tears in vain and while the truth of the slanders has not been proved, I am unable to come to Kamakura to say anything in my defence. Long is it now since I have been permitted to behold your face … But when, in the new harmony of our brotherly affection, it was arranged that I should go forth in the campaign against the Heike, since Kiso Yoshinaka was overthrown and I set forth to destroy the whole family, what hardships are there both by land and sea that I have not undergone? At times spurring my steed over the towering crags heedless of all danger, at times braving the perils of the winds and waves of the boundless ocean; careless whether my body should be lost in the depths of the sea to be a prey for the great fishes. Moreover my helmet and armour were my only pillow, the bending of the bow my only business, while I put away all thought of aught but appeasing the wrath of our ancestral spirits, the object of my long cherished desire … I pray you therefore to bring these things before Yoritomo at a suitable time, and to take such measures that he will perceive that I am guiltless and pardon me.[3]

Despite these heartfelt words, Yoshitsune did not appease Yoritomo. An imperial edict was issued 'to smite Yoshitsune'. The outlaw was pursued for four years, accompanied only by a few trusted retainers, including the ever-faithful Benkei. One of the most famous stories of this period, which is often retold in Japanese plays, describes the two fugitives trying to cross a heavily armed border between two Minamoto-friendly provinces. In disguise at the crossing were Benkei, dressed as a monk, and Yoshitsune, disguised as his servant. The checkpoint guards seemed convinced the pair were genuine pilgrims, but as they were being waved through, Yoshitsune stumbled and one of the guards seemed to recognise the ex-commander's face. The quick-thinking Benkei saved the day by beating Yoshitsune for not being more careful. This satisfied the border guards that Yoshitsune must be a servant, as no-one would dare to strike his master in this way.

Yoshitsune managed to get as far north as Mutsu, which at one time represented the frontier badlands where the first samurai battled against the Emishi. But one day he and his men found themselves surrounded by 500 enemy samurai horsemen and, seeing the day was lost, Yoshitsune committed *seppuku*. As he did so, Benkei vowed to hold off their attackers for as long as possible. He did so for quite some time, even after his body had been riddled with arrows. None of the attacking samurai were brave enough to move in to finish off the giant, who stood motionless and tall, leaning before them on his *naginata*. In the end, a horse galloped by Benkei and knocked him to the ground – the warrior monk had been dead for some time, propped up by his *naginata*, and standing guard for his master even in death.

So with this tragic end Yoshitsune's legacy was sealed. He was not rewarded with his rightful place as Minamoto warlord, but his name lived on as the wronged hero of the Genpei War, forever resigned to walk the lonely path of the wandering fugitive.

TOMOE GOZEN

Tomoe Gozen was also a samurai hero of the Genpei War: one of Yoshinaka's retainers who fought with him almost to the end. However, Gozen was a rarity on the battlefield – she was one of the few recorded examples of a female samurai.

Samurai men were, of course, allowed to marry, as well as take a mistress of samurai rank; in later samurai history, both women were subject to checks by the *daimyo*'s officials. The main role of a samurai's wife was to raise the family and manage the household. She was expected to follow Confucian law, which required her to be subservient to her husband, treat older family members with piety and look after her children with care. Nevertheless, samurai wives were also expected to fight, especially in the face of an invading army, and for this reason the wives and daughters of the samurai class were trained in the martial arts. According to the *bushidō* code, a woman could be taught to fight but had to remember her place:

> Bushidō being a teaching primarily intended for the masculine sex, the virtues it prized in women were naturally far from being distinctly feminine … Young girls, therefore, were taught to repress their feelings, to indurate their nerves, to manipulate weapons – especially the long-handled sword called naginata, so as to be able to hold their own against unexpected odds. Yet the primary motive for exercises of this martial character was not for use in the field; it was twofold – personal and domestic. Women, owning no suzerain of her own, formed her own bodyguard. With her weapon she guarded her domestic sanctity with as much zeal as her husband did his master's.[4]

The *naginata* was a long, curved blade attached to the end of a pole. It was almost exclusively used by the warrior monks before the Genpei War, but then also became the primary weapon of the foot soldier. The weapon's curved blade made it suited for cutting an opponent rather than impaling him, as one would do with a spear. The *naginata* was also something of a leveller on the battlefield, allowing lowly *ashigaru* foot soldiers the chance to unhorse a high-ranking enemy samurai.

During the period of medieval Japan, owning a *naginata* and knowing how to use it became pivotal for samurai women, especially those trapped behind besieged castle walls. At such times, women were expected to fight, regardless of their normal duties. This would often mean making the ammunition for arquebuses and cannons, tending to the wounded, and preparing enemy heads for the *daimyo* or *shōgun's* head-viewing ceremony. If the castle was overrun, the women would have to fight the invaders, as no quarter would be given to those inside. There are many instances in samurai history when an invading army stormed a castle and slaughtered all inside, regardless of age or gender: at the siege of Hara Castle in 1638, 125,000 samurai overran the stronghold and massacred the 27,000 starving men, women and children inside, many of whom were too weak to stand.

While the *bushidō* code recommended women stay behind closed doors while their men went off to fight, this was not always the case. Those few samurai women who actually made it outside the castle gates and onto the battlefield probably wore the normal warrior's *yoroi* armour over the top of the wide, skirt-like *hakama* trousers. As time went on, this armour would become more fitted, flexible and stronger to reflect the changing nature of samurai battle. There are no accounts of a samurai woman wearing a helmet or headgear, so it must be assumed that she went without one. If on horseback, a samurai woman probably also carried a bow, as was the case with Tomoe Gozen.

WARRIOR WOMAN

Gozen appears suddenly and unexpectedly in the *Heike Monogatari* as 'one of two beautiful girls' that Yoshinaka had brought with him from his home province of Shinano. It can therefore be assumed that the women had been with the commander throughout his campaign against the Taira. Yoshinaka had been highly successful in his war and had even expelled the enemy samurai from the imperial capital of Kyoto. But once there, Yoshinaka succumbed to hubris and seized control of the city for himself. When Yoshinaka's cousin and Minamoto clan commander, Yoritomo, heard of these exploits, he was honour-bound to send an army against him. Leading the force was Yoritomo's brother, Minamoto Yoshitsune.

After defeating Yoshinaka's army at the second Battle of the Uji Bridge in 1184, Yoshitsune marched on Kyoto and forced his enemy to flee the city. Yoshinaka rode away with only seven retainers, one of whom was Gozen. Yamabuki, the second of Yoshinaka's samurai woman, is reported as being sick and stayed in the capital to meet her fate. Gozen is thus described in the *Heike Monogatari*:

> Tomoe had long black hair and a fair complexion, and her face was very
> lovely; moreover she was a fearless rider whom neither the fiercest horse
> nor the roughest ground could dismay, and so dexterously did she handle

sword and bow that she was a match for a thousand warriors, and fit to meet either god or devil. Many times had she taken the field, armed at all points, and won matchless renown in encounters with the bravest captains, and so in this last fight, when all the others had been slain or had fled, among the last seven there rode Tomoe.[5]

Yoshinaka and his remaining samurai were soon caught by Yoshitsune's samurai and took their last stand. Gozen's presence at this point is notable, not just because of her apparent martial skills but also for her stubborn loyalty to her master, even though the group was outnumbered and clearly about to meet its end:

> But now they were reduced to but five survivors, and among these Tomoe still held her place. Calling her to him Kiso [Yoshinaka] said: 'As you are a woman, it were better that you now make your escape. I have made up my mind to die, either by the hand of the enemy or by mine own, and how would Yoshinaka be shamed if in his last fight he died with a woman?' Even at these strong words, however, Tomoe would not forsake him, but still feeling full of fight, she replied: 'Ah, for some bold warrior to match with, that Kiso might see how fine a death I can die.' And she drew aside her horse and waited. Presently Onda-no-Hachiro Moroshige of Musashi, a strong and valiant samurai, came riding up with thirty followers, and Tomoe, immediately dashing into them, flung herself upon Onda and grappling with him dragged him from his horse, pressed him calmly against the pommel of her saddle and cut off his head. Then stripping off her armour she fled away to the Eastern Provinces.[6]

There are many different stories about Gozen's life after the Genpei War. In some accounts she was attacked by one of Yoshinaka's surviving retainers, who then made her his concubine. In another she joined a nunnery and lived into peaceful old age. The most popular ending has Gozen committing suicide by jumping into the sea after hearing of Yoshinaka's death – a fitting end for a woman who was a match for any of her male opponents.

SAIGŌ TAKAMORI

While Minamoto Yoshiie was known as the first great samurai, Saigō Takamori was considered to be the last. His valour, bravery and honour marked not only the end of the samurai's power in Japan, but a new era for the country. This would become the modern age of Japan, dominated by advances in technology and armaments that would change the country from an inward-looking backwater into a global military power.

Saigō Takamori was born into a low-ranking samurai family in the Satsuma domain in 1828. He grew into a physically striking man with piercing eyes and a strong sense of samurai *bushidō*, especially the virtues of bravery and honour. An excellent swordsman, Takamori moved quickly through the samurai ranks, winning friends and influence along the way.

In 1867 Takamori and a number of other samurai dissatisfied with the *shōgun* forced his resignation and put a new emperor on the throne. The return to Japan of imperial rule was known to world history as the Meiji Restoration. In 1871 Takamori was eventually persuaded to play a part in the emperor's new government and took command of the imperial guard. He then helped disband the last provincial armies and open the way for a new national force. While Takamori did not support conscription, on the grounds that it would diminish the samurai's power, he did call for modernisation of the country's military.

Takamori also demanded that Japan attack Korea, as it had not recognised Meiji as the new emperor of Japan. He wanted to visit Korea as an envoy so he could provoke its government into killing him, thus giving Japan the excuse it needed to attack. But, while popular for a time, Takamori's plan was eventually rejected. This led him and a hundred of his officers in the Imperial Guard to resign.

After returning to his native Kagoshima, Takamori set up several swordfighting academies, which more than 20,000 disaffected samurai from all over Japan flocked to join. Takamori was not planning anything other than preparing men for military service, but the government in Tokyo was worried. It sent several warships to empty the Kagoshima arsenals in case of a rebellion. A group of Takamori's samurai reacted angrily to this, and on 29 January 1877 they took over the arsenals and began making weapons for themselves. Takamori was finally persuaded to lead this new rebel army, but he did so with a heavy heart.

There followed six months of full-scale warfare, with both sides relying heavily on the modern weapons of rifles and cannons. From the beginning, Takamori's army suffered disastrous defeats, and between February and September 1877 his numbers fell from 20,000 to just 400.

The final Battle of Shiroyama took place on 24 September 1877: Takamori's rebels had been forced back to Shiroyama Hill and, when their ammunition ran out, used bows and swords. Over 30,000 government troops mounted a siege, digging trenches, and using cannon and battleship artillery to bomb Takamori's position. Eventually, the imperial soldiers stormed the hill. This battle was perhaps the last stand of the samurai, who killed large numbers of the imperial force, untrained in close-quarter combat.

After one more retreat there were only forty samurai left and Takamori himself had been mortally wounded by a bullet. The remaining samurai made a last charge on horseback, but were mown down by the newest military technology to enter Japan – the American Gatling gun. Caught between the modernisation of his country and its inevitable eradication of the samurai, Takamori behaved honourably according to the *bushidō* code. He fought valiantly and, in defeat, took his own life.

NOTES

1 *Heike Monogatari*
2 Ibid.
3 Ibid.
4 *Bushidō: The Soul of Japan*
5 *Heike Monogatari*
6 Ibid.

8

Popular Culture

THE LAST SAMURAI MOVIE

Samurai warriors have been favourites for many years in TV shows,
cartoons, video games, books and movies, and the cult of the samurai
continues today. Usually these are stylised attempts to portray heroic
warriors obeying the *bushidō* code. This image of the stoic, honourable
samurai is a staple of popular culture, no matter how much the stereotype
may differ from the historical reality. One example is Hollywood's
The Last Samurai, with Tom Cruise as the virtuous meditative warrior.

The film opens with an aerial shot of Japan (which is actually New
Zealand, where it was filmed): 'They say Japan was made by a sword,' says
the narrator. 'I say, Japan was made by a handful of brave men, warriors,
willing to give their lives for what seems to have become a forgotten
word: honour.' The action starts with Nathan Algren (Cruise), a jaded
American ex-army officer who is recruited by the Meiji government
to train the new modernised Japanese army. It is needed, in particular,

139

to put down a rebellion led by Samurai leader, Moritsugu Katsumoto (Ken Watanabe). But Algren swaps sides, becomes a samurai and goes on to fight in the last ever samurai battle. In the end, Algren presents Katsumoto's sword to the emperor, who suddenly realises the importance of Japan's samurai traditions.

The movie is roughly based on Saigō Takamori, who has become Katsumoto in the film. The chronology has been changed to fit the story, and the American characters replace the French Military Mission, which helped the Japanese train their new army in the 1870s. As the movie is not claiming to be based on fact, it is arguably not fair to criticise it for historical inaccuracies. The storyline follows the standard Hollywood format and this makes the movie wholly predictable and implausible at times. Algren lives in Katsumoto's village for one winter, but in that time has achieved a mastery of samurai swordsmanship, become fluent in the language, and has attained a deep understanding of the complex *bushidō* code. Algren becomes the most honourable man standing, and by the end of the movie is able to teach the emperor a lesson about his country's samurai roots. As if underlining this sentiment, Cruise himself even appears to look slightly more Japanese than usual on the promotional posters.

Edward Zwick, one of *The Last Samurai* producers, said the movie had simplified Japanese history so Western audiences would understand it, but admitted that it had mythical and nostalgic overtones: 'The only thing one can do is hope that with a kind of immersion and some respectful understanding that what you come up with is a distillation, rather than a cliché.'

American critics felt the *The Last Samurai* had failed in this task and largely panned the movie, often branding it a Japanese *Dances with Wolves*. A review in *The Detroit News* wrote:

> *The Last Samurai* pretends to honor a culture, but all it's really interested
> in is cheap sentiment, big fights and, above all, star worship. It is a sham,
> and further, a shame.

Critics thought that the charge of style without substance also applied to the publicity for the movie's Los Angeles premiere. The advertisement sought 'beautiful Asian women willing to dress up and mingle in character ... to create the ambiance of ancient Japan, circa 1870's'.[1]

Ironically, the Japanese public was more forgiving and *The Last Samurai* did better business there. This was perhaps because the movie was an improvement on the older and even more historically inaccurate Hollywood samurai movies. Japanese movie reviewer Tomomi Katsuta told *The New York Times* that *The Last Samurai* was at least considered a step up from the American movies *Shōgun* and *Rising Sun*: 'Those films were humiliating for Japanese audiences. They didn't understand Japanese culture or the customs of the Japanese.' But Japanese critics were quick to condemn *The Last Samurai*'s pious, pure and philosophical character, Katsumoto: 'It set my teeth on edge,' said Katsuta.

The movie's strength lies in its battle scenes and it provides a reminder of the very real conflict occurring in Japan at the time. The samurai were being made obsolete by the country's modernisation and new weaponry; training to live and die honourably by the sword became futile in the face of a machine gun. The viewer is shown in graphic terms that there was no place for the samurai in modern warfare, which Japan itself had realised when it abolished the samurai class.

The Last Samurai was one of several Western samurai movies which gave the genre a rebirth in America, although this revival, which notably included *Kill Bill*, did not win critical approval in Japan. *Kill Bill* is Quentin Tarantino's homage to Japanese samurai theatre, a pastiche of B-movie motifs and revenge-thrillers with a storyline closely based on the 1973 Japanese film, *Lady Snowblood*. As the film's characters more closely resemble cartoon characters than human beings, it escaped criticism of its portrayal of samurai ideals, but Japanese critics bemoaned the further propagation of inaccurate samurai themes in popular culture. Japanese production manager, Ken Sugawa, told *The New York Times*:

> I think that many Japanese people understand Quentin Tarantino's aims. He wants to describe not real Japan and its culture, but the people and culture

in films such as yakuza and B-action movies. However, general Japanese audiences are not interested in what Mr. Tarantino finds interesting.[2]

While the debate continues about Hollywood's role in the historical recreation and cultural interpretation of foreign countries, one thing is certain: the samurai movies made in America were only ever made possible by the original samurai movies and television made in Japan itself.

SAMURAI IN JAPANESE POPULAR CULTURE

Japan's tradition of samurai TV, movies and theatre is called *jidaigeki*. *Jidaigeki* is a costume drama set during Japan's Edo Period and features the lives of various recurring characters, including samurai, villains, government officials, merchants, farmers and craftsmen. *Jidaigeki* is instantly recognisable by its characters, who follow set conventions: they wear heavy make-up, speak formal Japanese with an old-fashioned dialect, use catchphrases (such as 'it is a terrible world'), and can be easily identified by their appearance (villains are unshaven, unkempt and messy, while the heroes are neat and clean-cut).

The most famous *jidaigeki* character is Zatoichi, the subject of innumerable TV series and movies since 1962. Zatoichi is a blind masseur and gambler who travels the country, singing, performing music and playing dice. Zatoichi gambles by listening to whether the dice have fallen on an even or odd number, and he often extinguishes the candles in a room before uttering his catchphrase: 'darkness is my advantage'. But unbeknown to those who meet him, he is actually a master swordsman who fights injustice and protects the innocent wherever he goes.

Zatoichi belongs to a sub-group of *jidaigeki* called *chanbara*, Japanese swordfighting movies of a swashbuckling type. The *chanbara* genre began with the film *The Fight at Honno Temple*, made in 1908 by Shozo Makino, often considered the father of Japanese cinema. *Chanbara* usually follows the life of a disillusioned *rōnin* who is committed to spending the rest of his life travelling and fighting. Characters often experience a moral quandary centring on a conflict between what is right and what is required by the *bushidō* code, leading invariably to a series of swordfighting duels. Even when a *chanbara* character is ambushed by multiple foes, only one or two attack at a time, with the others waiting politely for their turn. The genre enjoyed its heyday in the 1960s and 1970s when the movies became increasingly violent and explicit, such as Kobayashi's *Seppuku* (1962).

SEVEN SAMURAI

The most famous director of *chanbara* films is Akira Kurosawa, who directed *Rashōmon*, *Throne of Blood*, *Yojimbo*, *The Hidden Fortress* and arguably the best-known samurai movie of all time: *Seven Samurai* (1954). The film has often been praised by Western directors and it inspired an American remake, *The Magnificent Seven*, a gunfighter movie set in the Wild West.

Seven Samurai begins in a small Japanese village under threat by marauding bandits. A village elder suggests hiring a group of samurai to protect them, but the villagers worry that they cannot afford it and their daughters would be at risk from the samurai's sexual advances. Realising they have no choice, a young villager travels to the city to recruit warriors. As the village has nothing with which to pay except food, the elder suggests looking for 'hungry samurai'. In the city, the young villager stumbles across one seemingly honourable samurai who is rescuing a child from a kidnapper. Before travelling to the village, the samurai, Kambei Shimada (Takashi Shimura), meets six other companions who agree to join him. After some initial reservations the villagers warm to the samurai, although it is revealed they have been responsible for killing travelling samurai in the past. A heated discussion among the seven follows this revelation, but it is pointed out that for many years farmers were victimised by the samurai class and so their actions are understandable. As time goes on, bonds between the farmers and samurai strengthen, including a romance between one warrior and a farmer's daughter.

The samurai go about defending the village – creating fortifications around it and even launching a pre-emptive strike on the bandits' hideout. The movie culminates in a battle in the village: the samurai seem to be winning, but the bandit leader takes refuge in a hut and shoots two of the warriors in the back. In the end, the bandits are all killed and the samurai victorious, but only three of them are left standing. In the last scene, the villagers happily go to work in the rice fields, seemingly indifferent to the samurai standing below the graves of their dead companions. The love interest turns her back on her warrior and runs off to join in the singing in the fields. Shimada sums up the situation: 'Again we are defeated. The farmers have won, not us.'

Seven Samurai raises an important point about the relationship between the samurai and those beneath them. The villagers have killed samurai in the past after being abused by them, and yet they have no choice but to turn to the warrior class for protection. In turn, the samurai are honour-bound under the *bushidō* code to do the right thing and to help the weak and oppressed. Yet when this task has been completed, the villagers, who are not educated or bound by the *bushidō* code, simply turn their backs on the samurai and get on with their farming. These *rōnin* are simply left to go on their way, condemned to wander aimlessly like so many others of the Edo Period.

Seven Samurai was Kurosawa's first samurai movie and set the benchmark for all others. It took the director a year to film and cost over $500,000 – a huge amount at that time, and four times the original budget. As such, the production company shut down the film three times, during which Kurosawa went fishing and reasoned that too much had been invested already for the movie to be cancelled. *Seven Samurai* went on to be Japan's highest-grossing movie of all time and Kurosawa's filmmaking has influenced the craft of many Western directors, including George Lucas, Robert Altman, Francis Ford Coppola, Steven Spielberg and Martin Scorsese.

Hideo Gosha is a less well-known director in the West, but his samurai films are often credited as being just as important as Kurosawa's for their contribution to the genre.

Gosha's movies present the antithesis of the Hollywood samurai – his warriors are portrayed as dark, broken and aggressive men who use their position of privilege for their own dubious self-interests. The best example of this character is Okada Izo (Shintaro Katsu) in *Hitokiri* (1969). Izo is a *rōnin* working as an assassin for Hanpeita Takechi (Tatsuya Nakadai), to whom he is fiercely loyal. Izo hopes to earn enough money and recognition to become a warrior of standing, but he is far from the samurai ideal – he cries and has no respect for his *katana*, let alone the *bushidō* code. In the end his loyalty, ambition and narrow-sightedness cause his downfall – he is betrayed by Takechi and sentenced to crucifixion. Before going to his death, Izo is told Takechi has also been sentenced to die by *seppuku*.

This theme of samurai plagued by the unforeseen consequences of their actions – usually performed out of loyalty to their master or clan – is further explored in the film *Goyokin* (1969). Samurai Magobei Wakizaka's (Tatsuya Nakadai) leader, Rokugo Tatewaki (Tetsuro Tanba), slaughters a group of innocent farmers to steal the gold they are transporting for the Tokugawa clan. Wakizaka agrees to keep silent as long as Tatewaki promises never to repeat his actions. But Tatewaki sends a *rōnin* after Wakizaka to assassinate him, although in the end he is talked out of it. In the final scene, a showdown takes place between Wakizaka and Tatewaki, who is continuing to kill innocents and take more gold. As with *Seven Samurai*, *Goyokin* questions the morality of the all-powerful samurai class and its hierarchical structure.

While the samurai are at the top of the Japanese class system, those inside the caste itself have to offer blind devotion to the *daimyo* and *shōgun* above them. This point is made at the end of *Goyokin* after both samurai struggle to pick up their swords to fight in a freezing blizzard. One says: 'We sit here and die in the cold, and what does the Shōgun do? He gets fatter in the heat.' It is this sentiment that has led many to call *Goyokin* an 'anti-samurai samurai movie', and it certainly does not disguise its criticisms. However, the movie is also a carefully thought-out study of the plight of the samurai at the end of their legacy: they are left with the echoes of the *bushidō* code, but without the context of warfare within which to use it.

NOTES

1   *The Detroit News*, 2003
2   *The New York Times,* 2004

Conclusion

It is one of the great ironies of samurai history that it was the warriors themselves who brought about their own downfall. Those late nineteenth-century clan leaders who fought to reinstate imperial rule soon faced the abolition of their own caste as a result. The subsequent suppression of the samurai class included the loss of their feudal domains, their rice stipend, their retainers, and then, in 1876, their swords. But the samurai clan leaders did not necessarily lose their power. As many samurai fell into obscurity, individual warriors who ruled over them took up positions of authority in the government and military. Here, they would bring the martial ideals of samurai *bushidō* to the global stage and apply them to the rising military conflicts of the industrial age.

Following the abolition of the samurai, Japan became a quaint curiosity for the foreigners now allowed to land on her shores. Genuine relics from a medieval society were of great interest to Western outsiders, who must have felt as though they had been transported back in time. Samurai swords and armour proved of particular interest, and often warriors who had faced starvation under the old regime found themselves wealthy samurai antique dealers to the West.

It was not just samurai artifacts and memorabilia that piqued foreign interest, though, for their customs and traditions continued to fascinate and horrify in equal measure. In 1868, British diplomat A.B. Mitford wrote a shocked eyewitness account of *seppuku*, where he described the 'hideous noise of the blood throbbing out of the inert heap before us'. But upon arriving home, Mitford also expressed genuine admiration for the ritual: 'We in this country are apt to look on *hara-kiri* as a barbarous and even theatrical form of suicide. It is nothing of the kind. It is indeed the sublimation of all those ideas of honour which constitute the very essence of chivalry.'

Seppuku as a punishment was made illegal in 1873, as Japan rapidly turned its back on archaic traditions and adopted modern technology in its army and navy. The Japanese military soon became a formidable new war machine, equipped with the latest armaments and eagerly anticipating overseas expansion. When conflicts against China and Russia did come at the end of the nineteenth century, it was impossible for newspapers to resist drawing comparisons with Japan's martial past. The tiny new power, which had decades earlier existed as an unacknowledged backwater at the end of the world, was now challenging two of the largest nations, displaying exactly the courage and fearlessness described on the first page of any *bushidō* manual.

Foreign interest in the *bushidō* ethos was sparked further by Inazō Nitobe's *Bushidō: The Soul of Japan* (1900). The book, written in English, was a great hit among overseas readers and compared aspects of samurai *bushidō* to medieval chivalry and the martial honour of Homer's *Iliad*. There was also another side to the *bushidō* ideals of honour in warfare, however, and it was the swaggering, bullish and reckless self-belief so often displayed by samurai warriors. Japan's military now appeared to be behaving in just this way and it caused consternation and anguish among foreign powers. In the early twentieth century, Japanese aggression in Taiwan and Korea became the focus of international concern about Japan's apparent lack of conscience over military oppression.

The *bushidō* themes of fearlessness, self-sacrifice and loyalty unto death were in full evidence by the time the Second World War began. Here,

Japanese soldiers were known for their blind bravery: they would charge towards enemy machine-gun fire wielding samurai swords; and fighter pilots willingly crashed their planes into enemy warships. Cheap samurai swords went into mass production so every soldier could have a samurai symbol of strength and solidarity. Suicidal resolve was strengthened with slogans and battle cries such as 'seven lives for Japan' and 'ten thousand years to the emperor'. As the *kamikaze* wind had wiped out the Mongol invaders of the thirteenth century, so it was hoped the *banzai* squadrons of the twentieth century would do the same.

The samurai tradition, on the other hand, had always had a dark side. It lauded honour and bravery, self-denial and chivalry, loyalty and self-sacrifice, but it was also a cult of death and suffering. It expected its warriors to kill themselves and to kill others, and to show no pity in either. The samurai wars were merciless contests which often ended in massacres of the defenceless and innocent, and this dark history spilled over into Japan's modern habits of warfare long after the samurai had been abolished. Japan's record of atrocity during the Second World War was by no means unique – the German invasion of the Soviet Union was an unimaginable slaughter, where Slavs and Jews were butchered as a matter of policy – but Japan's atrocities are similarly infamous. The Rape of Nanking in 1937 cost at least 200,000 lives and was an orgy of sadism. Japanese soldiers competed to see how quickly they could behead 100 victims with their swords, and the 'competition' was published in Japanese newspapers. Japanese war crimes continue to cause trouble between Japan and China today, and to darken the reputation of what is now a modern and enlightened state. In a way, the Second World War showed what happens when a warrior tradition turns poisonous. By the time the bombs landed on Hiroshima and Nagasaki, Japan's suicidal ethos had reached fever pitch and its people were starving.

National pride in its samurai past was heavily discouraged during the Allied occupation of Japan. The American administrators published texts condemning Japan martial history and, in particular, the symbol of the samurai sword. *Kendo* had been part of the school curriculum since 1911, but in 1945, fencing, swordplay and all forms of martial arts were banned.

It even became forbidden to use the word *bushidō*. It is telling that Akira Kurosawa, the legendary film director of *Seven Samurai* fame, had a 1945 samurai film banned by the American censor. The Supreme Commander of the Allied Powers prevented the release of *The Men Who Tread on the Tiger's Tail*, a feature about samurai heroes Yoshitsune and Benkei, because of its 'portrayal of feudal values'. The film was finally seen by the viewing public in 1952, towards the end of the occupation.

Following the departure of the occupying authorities, the samurai crept back into public consciousness through books, comics, theatre and, of course, *jidaigeki* television drama. As well as bringing samurai back to the fore, *jidaigeki* also introduced the warrior's shadowy counterpart – the ninja assassin. The ninja quickly gained popular appeal and became a rich source of material for pulp fiction and potboiler paperbacks. The actual existence of ninjas, also known as *shinobi*, is the subject of fierce historical debate, although it is generally acknowledged that stealth warriors were used during the samurai era for the purposes of spying and espionage.

By the time of Kurosawa's 1954 *Seven Samurai*, there was a rising feeling that Japan was once again able to cautiously acknowledge its samurai past. From the late 1960s onwards, *taiga* television dramas began celebrating the epic stories of the samurai legends – Minamoto Yoshitsune, Toyotomi Hideyoshi and Miyamoto Musashi among them. At the time of writing, a series on the villain of the Genpei War, Taira Kiyomori, was the latest *taiga* drama to be running on Japanese television. The true nature of the samurai warrior, an elusive and endlessly fascinating enigma, will hopefully continue to be the subject of drama, debate and discussion for many centuries to come.

Bibliography

Berry, Mary Elizabeth, *Hideyoshi* (Harvard University Press, 1982)

Bryant, Anthony J., *The Samurai* (Osprey, 1989)

Clearly, Thomas, *Training the Samurai Mind: A Bushidō Sourcebook* (Shambhala Publications, 2009)

Clements, Jonathan, *A Brief History of the Samurai* (Constable & Robinson, 2010)

Knoblock, John and Riegel, Jeffrey, *The Annals of Lu Buwei* (Stanford University Press, 2001)

McCullough, Helen Craig, *Taiheiki: A Chronicle of Medieval Japan* (Columbia University Press, 1959)

Musashi, Miyamoto, *The Book of Five Rings*

Nitobe, Inazō *Bushidō: The Soul of Japan*

Norman, F.J., *The Fighting Man of Japan* (Dover Publications, 2006)

Rankin, Andrew, *Seppuku: A History of Samurai Suicide* (Kodansha International Ltd, 2011)

Sadler, A.L., *Heike Monogatari* (Asiatic Society of Japan, 1918)

Sansom, George, *A History of Japan to 1334, 1334–1615 & 1615–1867* (Stanford University Press, 1961)

Sinclaire, Clive, *Samurai: The Weapons and Spirit of the Japanese Warrior* (Salamander Books, 2001)

Truman, Benjamin C. *The Field of Honor*

Tsunetomo, Yamamoto, *Hagakure: The Way of the Samurai*

Turnbull, Stephen, *The Samurai Sourcebook* (Cassell, 1998)

Turnbull, Stephen, *Samurai: A Military History* (Osprey, 1977)

Wilson, William Scott, *The Lone Samurai: The Life of Miyamoto Musashi* (Shambhala Publications, 2013)

Index

If you enjoyed this book, you may also be interested in …

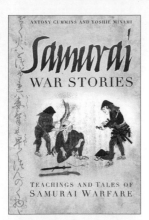

Samurai War Stories: Teachings and Tales of Samurai Warfare
ANTONY CUMMINS, YOSHIE MINAMI

Enter the world of seventeenth-century Japanese warfare and the warrior elite: the Samurai. This book features three major texts and include writings on three distinct military strata: the Samurai; the Ashigaru or foot soldier; and women in war. Narratives of actual battles and sieges are included in the texts, such as the famous Battle of Sekigahara. This collection is an invaluable resource that sheds new light on the world of the legendary Japanese warrior.

978 0 7524 9000 7

Iga and Koka Ninja Skills
ANTONY CUMMINS, YOSHIE MINAMI

Through patient and scholarly detective work, Antony Cummins and the Historical Ninjutsu Research Team have unearthed a Shinobi treasure. The eighteenth-century military historian Chikamatsu recorded the oral traditions of the Ninja and passed on those skills in lectures he gave at his Renpeido school of war in Owari domain during the early 1700s. Chikamatsu wrote specifically about the Shinobi of Iga and Koka, regions from which warriors were hired all over the land in the days of war. The lost scrolls are filled with unknown Shinobi teachings, skills.

978 0 7524 9362 6

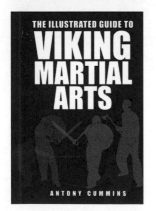

The Illustrated Guide to Viking Martial Arts
ANTONY CUMMINS

Martial Arts expert Antony Cummins reveals the hitherto hidden world of Viking hand-to-hand combat, employing the sword, the spear, the axe and the shield. Based upon a careful analysis of the Norse Sagas, the techniques described are recreated precisely, from knocking down a spear in mid-flight to the shield cleave. Illustrated with over 250 images, *The Illustrated Guide to Viking Martial Arts* in effect represents the earliest combat manual in the world. This insight into the warriors who were the scourge of Dark Age Europe is a feat of textual interpretation – and imagination.

978 0 7524 8060 2

Visit our website and discover thousands of other History Press books.

www.thehistorypress.co.uk